Thomas Schirrmacher

Racism

World Evangelical Alliance

International Institute for Religious Freedom
IIRF

The WEA Global Issues Series

Editors:

Geoff Tunnicliffe,
Secretary General, World Evangelical Alliance

Thomas Schirrmacher,
Director, International Institute for Religious Liberty and
Speaker for Human Rights of the World Evangelical Alliance

Volumes:

1. Thomas K. Johnson – Human Rights
2. Christine Schirrmacher – The Islamic View of Major Christian Teachings
3. Thomas Schirrmacher – May a Christian Go to Court?
4. Christine Schirrmacher – Islam and Society
5. Thomas Schirrmacher – The Persecution of Christians Concerns Us All
6. Christine Schirrmacher – Islam – An Introduction
7. Thomas K. Johnson – What Difference does the Trinity Make
8. Thomas Schirrmacher – Racism

"The WEA Global Issues Series is designed to provide thoughtful
and practical insights from an Evangelical Christian perspective into
some of the greatest challenges we face in the world.
I trust you will find this volume enriching and helpful in your Kingdom service."

Dr. Geoff Tunnicliffe, Secretary General, World Evangelical Alliance

Thomas Schirrmacher

Racism

With an essay by Richard Howell on Caste in India

Dr. Richard McClary, Translator
Patricia Foster, Proofreader
Dr. Thomas K. Johnson, Text editor

The WEA Global Issues Series
Volume 8

WIPF & STOCK · Eugene, Oregon

Verlag für Kultur und Wissenschaft
Culture and Science Publ.
Bonn 2012

RACISM
With an essay by Richard Howell on Caste in India

This edition published by Wipf and Stock Publishers in cooperation with Verlag für Kultur und Wissenschaft.

Wipf & Stock
An imprint of Wipf and Stock Publishers
199 W. 8th Avenue, Suite 3
Eugene OR, 97401
www.wipfandstock.com

ISBN 13: 978-1-62564-618-7

Manufactured in the U.S.A.

Content

The Bible and Global Social Problems 7

Preface (by Thomas K. Johnson) 9

I. Racism and its Refutation 11

1. What is Racism? 11

Excursus: With God there is no Favoritism! 13

Excursus: Important Bible passages directed against Racism 18

2. There are no human Races 19

Excursus: The Senselessness of Hitler's Thoughts on Race 22

3. 'Blacks,' 'Yellows,' 'Reds,' 'Whites' 26

Excursus: Ethiopians ("People of Cush") in the Old and New Testaments 31

4. IQ Racism 36

5. We are all 'MixedBreeds' 38

Excursus: Was the Old Testament Prohibition against Marriage to Non-
    Jews racist? 43

II. On the History of Racism and its Justification 45

1. The History of Racist Theories 45

Excursus: Evangelicals and Slavery 52

Excursus: The Death Penalty for Slave Traders in the Old Testament 54

2. Genocide 54

Excursus: Diversity of Cultures in the Bible 60

3. Racial Segregation 61

4. The Combination of Racism with other Factors 65

III. The Situation in Germany 69

1. Gypsies 69

2. Anti-Semitism 70

3. National Socialism 71

4. Right-wing Extremism in German-speaking Countries today 74

Excursus: The 'People' as a divine Order in Creation? 77

Internet Links and Bibliography 79

Dehumanizing Caste System (by Rev. Richard Howell) 95

Overcoming an Indian Form of Racism 95

Ontological Basis for Caste..96

Resistance to Caste...98

Intolerant Society 101

Democracy and Caste...102

Caste Divisions in Church..104

Survival of Caste 105

About the Author..109

Biography..109

Books by Thomas Schirrmacher in chronological order (With short
    commentaries)...110

The Bible and Global Social Problems

Thomas Schirrmacher's short, serious book on racism richly illustrates the multifaceted relationship of God's Word to our global social problems. God's Word, as preached by Dr. Schirrmacher, is obviously deep, prophetic social *criticism*, which extends beyond sinful actions to the thoughts and motives in the hearts and minds of people. Not only do we do really horrendous things to other people; our thoughts and theories about people are often reflections of our sin. Even the usual definitions of race flow from the blackness of sin. This needs to be exposed to the light of truth. I hope tears run down your face when you read both about the sin of racism as well as about the sinful theories people have taught.

But our hope is that God's Word, which we all must proclaim, will *contribute* something much more humane and godly to our many societies. Schirrmacher has told some of the great stories about how biblical ideas and the efforts of Christians have both restrained sin (and sinful theories) and in previous centuries even ended much of the slave trade. The biblical message, along with people moved by the biblical message, has made huge contributions in the past history of many cultures. Thank the Lord. But these great stories are not finished! Cry out to God, that this would happen again and again and again through the Body of Christ. Through God's people God's Word can contribute to a more humane future for many. Who knows what God might do through you?! The world needs the salt of God's Word carried by God's people.

This assumes that God's Word can *create* a new community, really a new humanity, that people who are reconciled to God by faith in Christ can also be reconciled to each other, so that different peoples can honestly love each other before God in Christ, by the power of the Holy Spirit. Let the Body of Christ become a place where people from all backgrounds and cultures are really at peace with each other and truly respect the God-given dignity of others, where the sin of racism is truly overcome. What we hope God's Word will contribute to our world should first be created within and among our churches, in our mission agencies, in our schools, in our seminaries, and in our families. Let the Word of God bear fruit among believers!

And it is my deep conviction that this entire discussion of racism and human dignity, with open Bibles in our hands, *correlates* with an anxious cry arising from the bottom of human consciousness: "What is wrong with us, that we do such terrible things? Who are we? Is human dignity real? Can we find courage in the face of such terrible evil? Is there salvation?"

The many quotations from the Bible found in this book, mostly in text boxes set apart from the rest of the book, provide the deepest answers to the questions running through the book. Indeed, one of the reasons to take the Bible so seriously is the way in which it addresses all the deepest cries, needs, and questions in all of life.

So read this book to learn, consider, weep bitterly, and then take action about racism. And along the way, notice the wide-ranging way in which the biblical message addresses all the problems of our broken world.

Thomas K. Johnson, Ph.D.

Preface

It might appear presumptuous to write in a way that 'puts in a nutshell' a phenomenon to which millions of people have fallen victim and which in the course of history has been used to justify genocide, slavery, and war as well as to justify centuries of all sorts of human rights violations. To reduce the terror of National Socialism and the mass execution of Jews and 'gypsies' to a couple of pages in a book, to cover slavery in colonial times and to mention the mass slaughter of Tutsis by Hutus in Rwanda simply does not appear commensurate with the sufferings of the victims of racism.

One could also write numerous pages about the many definitions of 'racism' and 'race' in order to do justice to all the literature on the subject that has been published. On the one hand, myriad opinions arise from missing or unclear basic principles regarding the definition of the terms. On the other hand, since we are dealing with something that has a lot to do with values and emotions, it is difficult to write neutrally about the topic from an academic point of view.

Still, it is only when one wants to grasp and refute racism 'in a nutshell' that the arguments against racism even have a chance. This is due to the fact that if only individuals who make the effort to burrow into the scholarly works of biologists, ethnologists, sociologists, and historians could be assured of refuting racism, then we would be rather helpless against racist propaganda.

I am, however, convinced of the fact that racism is suspect not only on account of its historical consequences but also because it is in opposition to Christian and humanist world views. In fact, everything that recent biology (in particular genetics) and cultural anthropology (including ethnology) have to say on the topic of race completely pulls the rug out from under racism.

The results of modern genetics, behavioral research, archaeology, linguistics, ethnology, and historical scholarship allow only one conclusion that representatives of belief in a Christian view of creation, regardless of whether they are in favor of evolutionary theory or not, have always supported: all of living humanity goes back to a common ancestor in Africa or in an adjacent part of Asia, namely the Middle East.[1] Furthermore, all people are genetically so closely related to each other that one can speak about

---

[1] Regarding the uncertainty as to whether humanity's origins lie in Africa or in the Middle East, comp. Luigi Luca Cavalli-Sforza, *Genes, Peoples, and Languages*, Berkeley (CA): Univ. of California Press, 2001, p. 7-61.

a single 'race,' if one speaks of 'race' at all. Racism is to be rejected because all people, in spite of their differences, have the same dignity. While the differences are what distinguish one person from another, they are certainly not what distinguish 'races' from each other.

As a teenager on vacation, I got lost in the port of Glasgow when our tour boat left the port without me on board. Left alone in a run-down area, a young 'black' boy took me in. Thanks to his hospitality and care, I spent the night in the small one-room quarters in which his poor family and their many children lived and slept. Their readiness to help was greater than that of many of the people I knew who had guest rooms. Two days later I was able to reach my parents by telephone. At that time I made a decision to treat people who look and live differently with the same normalcy and friendliness that the family that took me in did, although I was 'white' and 'rich.'

Since my parents had close contacts to the international Evangelical missions movement, church leaders were always coming and going, from Indonesia, Paraguay, and Gambia, as well as from other countries. As a small child I curiously touched the hair of Africans who thereafter gave technically oriented lectures. I grew up aware that people are very different, and yet all of them deserve respect.

Perhaps that was the reason why in addition to theology I enjoyed studying sociology and ethnology, the latter more generally referred to in the USA as cultural anthropology. Meanwhile I have investigated in my second dissertation, which was in cultural anthropology, the nonsensical theories of Hans Naumann and others regarding so-called "folk psychology." In my dissertation entitled *Hitler's War Religion* I investigated the devastating effects that occurred when people began to take a conglomeration of theories from race research and put it into blood-soaked practice.

Note: Since I consider the traditional separation of people according to skin color to be linguistically and *de facto* senseless, as will be documented in detail, I put these designations in single quotation marks whenever I use these designations to refer to people with this prescribed terminology ('black,' 'white').

I. Racism and its Refutation

1. What is Racism?

Definitions of Racism

The term 'racism' emerged in various European languages in the dispute with National Socialism that began at the end of the 1920s. The first definition of racism was formulated in 1940 by the American ethnologist Ruth Benedict: "... the dogma that one ethnic group is condemned by nature to congenital inferiority and another group is destined to congenital superiority. It is the dogma that the hope of civilization depends on eliminating some races and keeping others pure. It is the dogma that one race has carried progress with it throughout human history and can alone ensure future progress."[2]

What distinguishes this definition from modern definitions is that Benedict does not basically question the existence of human races. Rather, she views racism as a judgment on races that actually exist.

The longest standing definition of racism stems from the French sociologist Albert Memmi: "*Racism* is the generalized and absolutized judgment of actual or fictitious differences for the advantage of the persecutor and to the detriment of the victim, by which his privileges or his aggressions are justified."[3]

We see here that the differences can after all be of a fictitious nature, but that does not have to be the case. Newer definitions, however, correctly emphasize that the races that racism either elevates or vilifies are created by racism in the first place. Today most researchers involved in the study of racism hold that breaking humanity down into races is itself a racist theory, since race classification practically always serves to exclude people and to justify certain dependencies.[4]

---

[2] Ruth Benedict, *Race: Science and Politics*, New York: Modern Age Books 1940, p. 21.

[3] Translated from the French original, see also Albert Memmi, *Racism*, Minneapolis (MN): University of Minnesota Press, 1999.

[4] According to, for instance, Heidrun Kaupen-Haas/Christian Saller, *Wissenschaftlicher Rassismus: Analysen einer Kontinuität in den Human-Naturwissenschaften*, Frankfurt: Campus 1999, p. 65ff.

Three newer Definitions of Racism

"To attempt a short formulation, we might say that racism exists when one ethnic group or historical collectivity dominates, excludes, or seeks to eliminate another on the basis of differences that it believes to be hereditary and unalterable."[5]

"Racism is the belief that peoples, via hereditary features, differ in social value and make specific groups superior or inferior to others."[6]

"Racism includes ideologies and forms of practice on the basis of the construction of people groups as ancestral and descendent communities, to which collective features are ascribed and that implicitly or explicitly evaluate and interpret such features as unable to be changed or only able to be changed with difficulty."[7]

We, therefore, find two basic elements in racism:

1. the construction of ancestral groupings with alleged common features;
2. the evaluation of these groups and differences for the utility of the racists and for the detriment of the victims, thereby legitimizing privileges and aggression.

Therefore, the core of racism, in comparison to other ideologies that are used to oppress people (such as conceptions of class, religion, or disdain for the handicapped) is that what is different in the other person *is based on the individual's biological ancestry and is, therefore, unalterable.* "One can speak of the existence of a racist attitude or ideology if differences that otherwise are seen as ethno-cultural are declared to be innate, indelible, and unalterable."[8] In racism an alleged natural or God-given immutable system of domination serves to justify discrimination, exclusion, oppression, persecution or annihilation of people groups.

Two Strands of Argumentation against Racism

For reasons mentioned, one must argue on two levels against Racism.

Firstly, even proven differences between human races say nothing about the equal dignity everyone has. Skin color, body size, and IQ say nothing about who is valuable and who is not, and they give no one the right to oppress other people.

---

[5]   George M. Fredrickson, *Racism: A Short History*, Princeton: Princeton University Press, 2002, p. 170.

[6]   Declaration of Schlaining, par. 14 (see the bibliography).

[7]   Johannes Zerger, *Was ist Rassismus?* Göttingen: Lamuv 1997, p. 81.

[8]   Fredrickson, p. 13.

Secondly, there is no evidence for the assumption that there are such bio-logical differences between distinguishable races in the first place. It is not possible to assign people's appearance or behavior to biological ancestral groups with hereditarily determined similarities, and it is not possible to map any external features to their behavior or their character.

The second point should actually suffice. This is due to the fact that if there are no human 'races,' racism is always false. Why? Because it is impossible. And yet, racism, unfortunately, repeatedly constructs new 'races,' such that the first level argumentation basically has to be repeat-edly brought forth.

While the scientific evidence for the fact that there are no races increases with every decade, up until the present it is common to utilize ancient and frequently refuted divisions according to skin color in the absence of an alternative. Leading encyclopedias explain under the 'racism' heading that there is no such thing as races, only to then nonchalantly continue to refer to the differentiation under the 'race' heading or the headings of these in-dividual 'races.'

Excursus: With God there is no Favoritism!

The widely attested statement that when we make decisions we should show "no partiality" (Deuteronomy 1:17; II Chronicles 19:7; Proverbs 18:5; 24:23; Job 13:10; Ephesians 6:9; Colossians 3:25), because God him-self knows no partiality (e.g., Deuteronomy 10:17-18), means that only wicked judges show partiality (Isaiah 3:9). For that purpose James writes: "If you really keep the royal law found in Scripture, 'Love your neighbor as yourself,' you are doing right. But if you show favoritism, you sin and are convicted by the law as lawbreakers . . . Speak and act as those who are going to be judged by the law that gives freedom . . . (James 2:8-12).

There are numerous Forms of Racism

Racism is found in everyday life as well as in politics and scholarship. It ranges from prejudices and discrimination, slavery and racial segregation all the way to pogroms, forced displacement, ethnic cleansing, and geno-cide. The most extreme form up until now has been the industrial destruc-tion of the Jews under the Third Reich.

Eight different historical and present day Examples of Racism

Germany and Europe: Exhibitions of People in Zoos. The heyday of exhibiting people occurred between 1870 and 1940. This involved exhibit-ing non-European peoples in zoos, in circuses, and in special exhibitions.

During this time there were over 300 such groups in Germany, which consisted of groups of family size all the way up to groups of 50 people. What was well known were the areas in the Hagenbeck Zoo in Hamburg for Beduins, Somalians, or Eskimos. The true living conditions of these peoples were not shown. Rather, the penchant was for the clichés the public wanted to see.

Uganda: The forced Displacement of Indians. In 1972 the dictatorial government, with the support of the black African population, began to expel 80,000 Indians. Indians made up 1% of the population, but they accounted for 50% of the doctors and 80% of the business people in the country.

Soviet Union: Contempt for "Blacks." In the 1970's, at the expense of the Soviet Union, black Africans trained for the war of liberation in South Africa in camps near Moscow. When they were on leave and approached and spoke to Russian women, they were beaten up or arrested by the police.

South Africa: Racial Segregation. From 1948-1990 'whites' were not allowed to marry 'blacks,' 'Indians' (Asians, namely 'colored') or people of mixed race. The four groups mentioned had to live in separate housing complexes, go to separate schools and universities, use separate hospitals, means of transportation, toilets, and beaches, whereby the facilities for the 'whites' were naturally always better equipped. Only 4 million 'whites' had the right to vote, while 18 million blacks and others were left without the right to vote.

Rwanda: Tutsi Genocide. Between April and July 1994 somewhere between approximately 800,000 and 1 million people were killed within 100 days by members of the army, the police, and the civil population from within the Hutu majority. This action killed 75% of the Tutsis living in Rwanda.

USA: Was Adam 'white' or 'black'? Racist militias in the USA are convinced that Adam and Eve were white and only whites descend from them. Elijah Mohammed, the founder of the Nation of Islam, which was the American organization of 'Black Islam,' represented the idea that Allah created Adam black. Both groups thought that the other races emerged from commingling with animals.

Saudi Arabia: Exploitation of Filipinos. It is primarily Filipinos, either Muslim or Catholic, who do the dirty work for the many rich Saudis. They are in part housed and treated inhumanely, and their rights are handled in a bad way since they can be deported at any time. Additionally, Filipinos are often prepared to accept each and every job, because at home large families live off of the money they transfer back home.

Germany: the NDP (National Democratic Party of Germany) on Africa. "In actuality . . . all aid to developing countries is a giant swindle! Nothing can 'develop' in Africa that would equate to what one has in European terms. The truth is that everything that is found on the Black Continent with respect to civilization was created by whites. And there, where white men are not or no longer found, nothing works – things are that simple . . . The tax monies for foreign aid end up being bribes in the pockets of Negro chieftains . . ."[9] "Whoever indiscriminately speaks about 'people' and does not look at Germans should also not be shocked if he sees poverty stricken German retirees fishing for returnable bottles in garbage cans, while behind him stands a large oriental family fed by the state or an arrogant, affluent Negro stalking around! For whomever these are just undifferentiated 'people,' such a person is no longer capable of recognizing the screaming injustice of this everyday scene in the 'multi-colored Federal Republic of Germany'".[10]

Thereby, it is worth noting that racism is older than the term racism itself. It is older than every 'racial doctrine' and always occurs when people declare other groups to be a biologically common group that is subordinate, less civilized, lazier, or more dangerous. For this reason the United Nations defines "race discrimination" in the International Convention on the Elimination of All Forms of Racial Discrimination[11] of 1965 as "any distinction, exclusion, restriction or preference based on race, color, descent, or national or ethnic origin which has the purpose or effect of nullifying or impairing the recognition, enjoyment or exercise, on an equal footing, of human rights and fundamental freedoms in the political, economic, social, cultural or any other field of public life."

It should be mentioned in addition that there is not only one racism. Rather, there are other respective forms that it takes on *according to who incites it and against whom it is directed*. Racist movements always have a national or cultural characteristic, and they are strongly differentiated according to which group uses racism to fight which another group. ". . . wherever we find racism, we discover that it is historically specific, ac-

---

[9]   2007 Annual Report of the Berlin Office for the Protection of the Constitution, Berlin, p. 79 with quotes from the NPD Baden-Württemberg party homepage (July 3, 2007), see the bibliography.

[10]   Homepage of the NPD Party, May 10, 2007, quoted in the 2007 Annual Report of the Berlin Office for the Protection of the Constitution, Berlin, p. 77.

[11]   Http://www2.ohchr.org/english/law/pdf/cerd.pdf.

cording to the specific era, according to the particular culture, and according to the distinct societal form in which it arises. These respective specific differences need to be analyzed. When we speak about a concrete societal reality, we should, therefore, speak about racisms and not racism."[12]

The major and minor Racism of the 'Races'

The most basic form of racism acts on the assumption of major races of humanity and scorns and battles against 'blacks' (the most widespread type of racism throughout history and into the present), 'reds' (e.g., in Brazil), 'yellows' (e.g., in Uganda) and 'whites' (e.g., in Zimbabwe).

However, under racism one also includes the oppression of each small ethnic group or of whichever groups that the racist defines as belonging together.

If contempt by a 'major race' is already baseless, then it applies all the more because as a result of history most peoples are already mixed breeds. It would be saying too much to maintain that one could, for instance, biologically distinguish between Teutons and Jews, German and French, Catholic Irish and Protestant British from Northern Ireland, or Walloons and Flemish from Belgium, to just look at a few European examples.

If I am surveying everything correctly, there are three types of racism which internationally are the most widespread and which have over the centuries been able to be pursued. One stands for 'major' racism, and two stand for the 'minor type:

The three most widespread Types of Racism that are also international

The defamation and fight against or oppression of

1. **'Blacks'** (or of people who have a darker skin color than oneself) – they are allegedly dumb, barbarian and uncivilized;

2. **Jews** – they are allegedly devious, greedy, and domineering;

3. **'Gypsies'** – also called 'Roma,' they are allegedly asocial and thievish.

Other Terms

In the racial setting, there are often related terms that are used. They are to be outlined in the following.

---

[12]   Stuart Hall, „Rassismus als ideologischer Diskurs", in: Nora Räthzel (ed.), *Theorien über Rassismus*, Hamburg: Argument-Verlag 2000, p.11.

Everyday racism: Racism in everyday situations. The individual taking the racist action cannot offer an ideological justification, since the idea of the superiority of his own group is of such a second nature that the person takes the discrimination that follows from it to be normal and logical or not even noticed any longer.

Anti-Semitism: Hatred for Jews (and not for Semites in general), see pp. 70-71.

Anti-Zionism: Hatred for the modern Jewish state of Israel in Palestine. It is a special form of anti-Semitism, see p. 65 and 71.

Anti-Gypsyism: a technical term based on 'anti-Semitism' for hostility towards gypsies, see pp. 69-70.

Hatred of Foreigners: "Hatred of foreigners is first of all directed against the status of foreign nationality. Over the course of time this characteristic of being a non-native is intensified by ascribing negative characteristics that are possibly noticeable over generations in the people concerned. While racism in the narrower, biologically argued sense is based on the alleged inalterable ascription of features, this attitude can weaken with time. Where formerly certain people and groups were looked upon as foreign, they lose their stigma and are then perceived as 'accepted' and 'local.'[13]

Ethnocentrism: This is a fixation on one's own cultural context, which means exchanging the worldview one has of one's own culture with reality. In contrast to racism, ethnocentrism desires or forces the assimilation of others.

Xenophobia: a negative attitude and behavior against people and groups and outsiders of all types who are alien and different. Xenophobes hate the language, culture, clothing, and nationalities of others. Racism, on the other hand, hates the 'race' and 'descent,' whereby both naturally can go hand in hand. They mostly do, but it does not have to be the case.

Racial segregation: see pp. 61ff.

Racial discrimination: see p. 13-15.

---

[13] Federal Commission against Racism, www.ekr-cfr.ch/themen/00023/00028/index.html?lang=de.

Excursus: Important Bible passages directed against Racism

Acts 17:26-28a: "From one man he made every nation of men, that they should inhabit the whole earth; and he determined the times set for them and the exact places where they should live. God did this so that men would seek him and perhaps reach out for him and find him, though he is not far from each one of us. 'For in him we live and move and have our being.'"

Genesis 1:26-28: "Then God said, 'Let us make man in our image, in our likeness, . . . So God created man in his own image, in the image of God he created him; male and female he created them. God blessed them and said to them, 'Be fruitful and increase in number; fill the earth . . .'"

Genesis 5:1-2: "This is the written account of Adam's line. When God created man, he made him in the likeness of God. He created them male and female and blessed them. And when they were created, he called them 'man.'"

1 Corinthians 15: 21-22: "For since death came through a man, the resurrection of the dead comes also through a man. For as in Adam all die, so in Christ all will be made alive."

Philippians 2:3-5: "Do nothing out of selfish ambition or vain conceit, but in humility consider others better than yourselves. Each of you should look not only to your own interests, but also to the interests of others. Your attitude should be the same as that of Christ Jesus . . ."

1 Samuel 16:7 (God to the prophet Samuel): "But the LORD said to Samuel, 'Do not consider his appearance or his height, for I have rejected him. The LORD does not look at the things man looks at. Man looks at the outward appearance, but the LORD looks at the heart.'"

Ephesians 2:14-18: (about Jews and pagans): "For he himself is our peace, who has made the two one and has destroyed the barrier, the dividing wall of hostility, by abolishing in his flesh the law with its commandments and regulations. His purpose was to create in himself one new man out of the two, thus making peace, and in this one body to reconcile both of them to God through the cross, by which he put to death their hostility. He came and preached peace to you who were far away and peace to those who were near. For through him we both have access to the Father by one Spirit."

2. There are no human Races

'Race' in Biology

How does biology nowadays use the term 'race'? The answer is clear: 'race' is now only used for plants that are raised by man as well as for productive livestock and pets. In these cases man breeds for particular characteristics and prevents the mixing of races by controlling breeding. This would be impossible to do with people. For wild animals and wild plants the term 'race' is practically no longer used.

In order to distinguish between biological species – which is clearly defined by the limitations of cross breeding – the term conspecies or subspecies gradually arose for plant 'forms' and 'varieties,' which, however, were for a long time not as clearly set down as the species and the hierarchical terms that were established with them.

All the people in the world can be 'crossed' with each other. What that means is that principally every man who is potent can have a child with every woman capable of bearing children. This is an unmistakable indication that in the case of people we are speaking of one and the same species. The United Nations has aptly laid this down legally, which by the way is an astonishing recovery of the Christian tradition: "All human beings belong to a single species and are descended from a common stock. They are born equal in dignity and rights and all form an integral part of humanity".[14] In the *Lexikon der Biologie* (*Encyclopedia of Biology*) one reads the following: "In the study of race within anthropology the term 'race' was used for the classification of people groups at various levels below the species *homo sapiens*, whereby only the so-called geographic major races (Caucasian, Mongoloid, Negroid) could have corresponded to the status of sub-species. Different populations and molecular-genetic investigations indicate, however, that the division of mankind into 'races' has no genetic basis."[15]

Biology Professor Ulrich Kattmann from Oldenburg has represented the view in numerous publications that the term race in biology has generally become as obsolete as it has with reference to people. "The critique against the concept of races of mankind is often met with misunderstanding and resistance from the biological side, since it is thought that the task of the

---

[14] Article 1 of the "Declaration on Race and Race Prejudice," see http://www2.ohchr.org/english/law/race.htm.

[15] *Lexikon der Biologie*, vol. 11, Heidelberg: Spektrum Akademischer Verlag 2003, p. 421 (Article entitled „Rasse").

term race as a general biological principle is infringed upon: race classification is a common procedure in all of biology . . . Man has no exceptional position and is, therefore, to be treated as all other animal species. The concept of race is necessary for an understanding of animal species. The concept of race is required for an understanding of evolution . . . The author admits that he himself thought this way for a long time . . . Detailed analysis shows, however, that none of the arguments for holding to a concept of races among mankind is biologically valid. First of all, it has been observed that the term 'race' in zoology has to the greatest extent become obsolete and is only extensively used by anthropologists and household pet researchers . . . The sole object range in which 'race' is used as a technical term has to do with varieties of household pets . . . natural populations are, however, genetically manifold and in no way are they comparable to household differentiated populations that are geographically clearly distinguished and are zoologically designated as sub-species. The subdivision of species into sub-species or even more precise categories is by no means an obligatory biological principle. The zoological classification is only mandatory at the species level: Every procreating organism that requires two parents necessarily belongs to a biological species, which is defined as a reproductive community . . . With people the diversity within and between the populations is so complex that it is inexpedient to further subdivide this species . . . The concept of race is simply unfit to capture the genetic differences of people in their individual and geographic diversity."[16]

Despite great efforts, Races have not been found

The term 'race' is one of the most successful ideas of modernity. Prior to 1400 it was unknown in all its components, and in the 18th century it developed gradually. From that time onward, and up until the middle of the 20th century, there was hardly anyone who doubted the existence of clearly distinguishable major human races, although there had never been a halfway acknowledged division of such races.

From 1850 until about 1950, one can speak of the heyday of anthropological race measurement techniques. Skin color tables, bone measurements, body size, cranial measurements, and numeric ratios were the order of the day. There was little that was not measured and categorized with great effort throughout the entire world. If there ever had been the possibility of dividing humanity into manageable and distinguishable races, it would have had to have been found.

---

[16] Ulrich   Kattmann,   "Rassismus,   Biologie   und   Rassenlehre,"   in: www.shoa.de/content/view/368/96/.

This is, however, the way in which innumerable race classification theories came about, and the work associated with it was shoddily conducted. This was demonstrated primarily by Stephen Jay Gould in his classic text *The Mismeasure of Man*. The shoddiness of the work conducted meant that the data was bent to shape and interpreted until the desired result was achieved. In the beginning it was the size of the brain that was taken as the indication of races and their value. When it, however, became clear that Eskimos, Laplanders, Malays, and Tartars had the largest brains, this feature was dropped.[17] It had anyway been known for a long time that the size of the brain and intelligence are not automatically associated, with the result that good excuses were able to be made about the data.

There was never a generally accepted division of people into races. Rather, there were always new and changing suggestions that many researchers even rescinded within their own lifetimes as scientists.[18] This also applies to the Third Reich, in which completely contradictory race classifications competed with each other.

This epoch of measurement techniques moved into a period of critique. Its first representatives would have been able to pull the foundation out from under racism after World War I had one just listened to them. The most important elements of critique were:

1. Hereditary characteristics and environmental characteristics cannot be adequately distinguished from each other. Before measurement results can be compared, it must be proven that they are hereditary and remain constant over many generations.

2. Measurements feign a juxtaposition of races, although the world population demonstrates a sliding continuum of different population mixes.

3. Every researcher establishes his own typology.

4. The typologies are not substantiated in field research conducted on site. It is so simple to place a photograph of a typical 'German' next to the photograph of a typical 'Russian' in an atlas, but it is difficult to find *the* German in Germany and *the* Russian in Russia. It is simply the case that due to thousands of years of trading relationships, migrations, streams of refugees, wars and marriages out of love, we are mixed breeds across all cultures.

---

[17]   Stephen Jay Gould, *Der falsch vermessene Mensch (*English: *The Mismeasure of Man)*, Frankfurt: Suhrkamp, 1994², p. 88.

[18]   See in part, Gould, *Mensch.*

5.   Awareness has increased more and more that the differences people have in language, culture, or religion cannot be attached to biological settings or genes. Rather, each one of them has a long cultural history, into which each individual gradually grows through socialization. "The classical argumentation of biological determinists fails because all characteristics, which they call upon to distinguish between groups, are normally the products of cultural development."[19]

When for instance all the children in a village in Africa play together in the street, grow up, and learn from each other with little school education, they will tend to be characterized by the acceptance of knowledge from those who are bigger and stronger. This is due to the fact that it is always the older and stronger children who set the tone. As a result of this, the child will also be shaped by learning via classroom teaching and reciting what he or she has learned. If the same child from the same village were to grow up with parents who are attuned to well structured formal education, and the child experiences a good classroom education, he would, as is common in Germany, no longer be raised by older children and determined by that situation. Rather, he would be shaped early by his relationship with adults, who want him to grow into a situation where he is self-reliant. The result is the same as in Germany. And vice versa: a German child, who as a baby is adopted in a poor African village, would develop the same learning behavior as an African child there.

Excursus: The Senselessness of Hitler's Thoughts on Race

Since race played such a central role in Hitler's thinking,[20] it is amazing that Hitler had such a vague definition of race, and he practically never addressed in any detail the question of race or race classification. He never admitted that any special school of racial thought was correct, and just as the entire racial movement, he did not distinguish between terms such as 'German,' 'Germanic,' 'Aryan,' or 'Nordic,' or between 'race,' 'folk,' 'fatherland,' or 'blood,' and he did not even once mention the races found in Hans F. K. Günther's quasi-official racial doctrines. What was at stake was to put "the scientific insights of racial doctrine" into practice. When it came to concrete supporting documents, it was Hitler's own observations

---

[19]   Gould, p. 360.

[20]   All documentation for the following section is found in Thomas Schirrmacher, *Hitlers Kriegsreligion: Die Verankerung der Weltanschauung Hitlers in seiner religiösen Begrifflichkeit und seinem Gottesbild*, 2 vols., Bonn: VKW 2007, vol. 1., pp. 246-258 and vol. 2, pp. 352-381.

that allowed him to recognize who belonged to which race and which race brought forth which culture.

When Hitler, for instance, wrote: "The racially pure Teuton who has remained unmixed on the American continent has risen up to become the ruler of the same," it can hardly be deciphered whether he means the Teutons in America who are the descendents of Germans, Northern Europeans, European immigrants, or the white race in general. Hitler himself had primarily propagated the term 'Aryan' through his use of the word in *Mein Kampf*. It underscores what was just said to mention that in 1935 the government of the Reich had attempted unsuccessfully to replace 'Aryan' by 'German-blooded.'

Lawrence Birken has correctly pointed out that these generally persistent statements made in Hitler's racial doctrine were the reason why completely varying racial doctrines among National Socialists could all find a reference point in Hitler.[21]

In National Socialism and in its literature completely contradictory concepts of race competed with each other. Were one to follow Günther's racial types, the question would arise as to where the actual Nordic race is even supposed to be living. The Nationalistic Socialistic educational theoretician Ernst Krieg was even of the opinion that race is rather acquired and conveyed by folk discipline. Next to this are many inconsistencies: if it had to do with recognizing external racial features, then it would be the case that Danes, Norwegians, and members of hostile nations had a higher racial value.

Hitler did not attach race to lineage and appearance as, for instance, Himmler did. Rather, Hitler attached race to leadership abilities demonstrated in practice. Goebbels also did this. Race was recognized in proving oneself, for instance in war or in leadership tasks, but not in outward appearance. At this point, Hitler's teaching of great character played a central role as the highest display of race. This is how Hitler's statement was reported on in 1942: "The racial struggle does not have to erupt if people are not chosen according to their external appearance but rather according to their ability to prove themselves. Appearance and nature often take separate paths. One can make a selection according to external appearances or one can make it, as the party does, according to fitness for life." Hitler's racial understanding is basically no longer a biological concept of race. Hitler recognized races and higher order value within a race on the basis of

---

[21] Lawrence Birken, *Hitler as Philosopher: Remnants of the Enlightenment in National Socialism*, Westport: Praeger 1995, pp. 57-60.

how people responded to his 'idea' and whether they were ready to fight, that is to say, put their worldview into practice in a death defying manner!

It is for this reason that Hitler also was in favor of making a selection among siblings and was rather generous to recognize Aryan features in half-Jews or quarter-Jews. Precisely this aspect was a strong indicator that Hitler took people's racial affiliation into account and that he could not and did not want to view them according to some scientific approach. Finally, it is for this reason that Hitler was able to place members of other races higher than Germans. He did this, for instance, in 1928 when he said: "An Anatolian farmer has more value than a German man of letters." And he was convinced that the "Japanese, Chinese and Islamic peoples are always closer to us" than "the French."

'Races' have been refuted by Genetics

Recent genetic investigations from around the world have brought to light the astonishing genetic similarity of all people, as well as, however, the striking commingling of the gene pool. At the DNA level all people are of *one* race, not of several. "The results of modern genetics have unobjectionably demonstrated that there are no different human races, and rather that there is only one species of mankind."[22] The genetic differences between people within one 'race' are on average greater than the genetic differences between different 'races.' "Modern DNA analysis, which has determined that genes do not carry any weight at all and yet code the visible differences, supports the viewpoint of many experts (in particular ethnologists and sociologists) that the term 'race' no longer serves a scientific purpose outside of biology and for that reason should be avoided."[23]

"Racists are still convinced that biological traits also determine differences in behavior, character, temperament, and with respect to intelligence. Modern genetic research demonstrates the opposite. Such research shows that cultural differences between groups cannot have biological causes. It is now known that human behavior, just as intelligence, is extremely strongly shaped by varying social conditions and significantly the product of culture, which is to say that it is learned."[24]

The most prominent human geneticist in the world, Luigi Cavalli-Sforza, who conducts research in the United States and in Italy and who has domi-

---

[22] Nicht „Rassen" schaffen Rassismus, sondern Rassismus schafft „Rassen", http://www.ekr-cfr.ch/themen/00023/index.html?lang=de.

[23] Willi Stegner (ed.), *Taschenatlas Völker und Sprachen*, Gotha: Klett-Perthes 2006, p. 16.

[24] Stegner, p. 16.

nated the field for 30 years, has submitted a comprehensive gene atlas, in which he analyzed people from all regions of the world on the basis of numerous genetic indicators. He demonstrates that external differences such as skin color and hair color, hair structure and nasal shapes are only adaptations to different climate and nutritional conditions, and that they are determined by a smallish sub-group of genes. Viewed genetically, in principle any group all the way down to the residents of a small village can be differentiated from other people. This means that among humans the genetic diversity is so large that it is zoologically inappropriate to take people as a biological species and subdivide them. This argument was used in 1871 by none other than Charles Darwin, who had no knowledge of modern genetics, in his book about the descent of man.

Statistically, the genetic difference between randomly chosen Africans and Europeans is only 15% greater than that between people from one and the same village.

A new study from 2008 takes the discussion further: "Just how rich in diversity is the human genome? And where did our direct ancestors live? Precisely these questions can now be answered with a global map of human genetic variation. With more exactness than ever before, scientists can now reconstruct via genetic variation human migratory movements and the genetic differences within individual people groups. The study, which has been published in the technical journal "Nature," is based on a combination of different methods for making genetic comparisons. "Scientists . . . sifted through the DNA of 485 people from 29 different populations and five continents and compared three types of genetic variation . . . 'Now that we possess the technology to examine thousands and even hundreds of thousands of genetic markers, we can conclude in better detail than ever before what the relationships are between human populations and what the former migrations were.' . . . People of African descent are genetically the most differentiated, followed by inhabitants of the Near East, Asians, and Europeans. The smallest range of variation was discovered by researchers to be among the original inhabitants of the Americas."[25]

The Example of Blood Groups

Blood group systems have been globally researched for a considerable length of time. This also applies to the way blood group systems hereditarily behave. Blood group systems are found throughout all alleged races and

---

[25] „Karte enthüllt genetische Vielfalt der Völker: Genvarianten spiegeln Wanderungsbewegungen des Menschen wider", www.scinexx.de/wissen-aktuell-7846-2008-02-22.html.

peoples, but only their percentage of distribution is varied. This applies to "blood groups" and to "rhesus factors," but it also applies to unknown blood characteristics such as the HLA group of antigens (human leucocyte antigen), which play a role in organ transplants. As far as the rhesus factor or HLA group antigens are concerned, Europeans and Africans are closest to each other and together differentiate themselves from Asians, Eskimos, and Indians.

For this reason every person can have blood donated for him or her by anyone who has a matching blood group, regardless of whether that person is a European, Asian, or Latin American. A so-called 'universal donor' with blood type 0 (Bloodtype 0, rhesus negative) can give blood to any person, regardless of ethnicity!

The Genetics of the 'white' Race

Genetic investigations confirm what linguistic science in a similar manner has always known. That is the fact that Indians are not related to other Asians, but rather to Europeans. It is for this reason that one speaks of Indo-Europeans. What is new, however, is the realization that this is also the case for Indians whose skin color is significantly darker than that of Europeans.

Genetic research shows that also in the case of blond Northern Europeans there are, genetically speaking, many ancestors detectable from Asia. These allegedly remote peoples are also mixed breeds consisting of natives and those who are non-natives and have immigrated from afar.

3. 'Blacks,' 'Yellows,' 'Reds,' 'Whites'

Three major Races of Humanity?

If there ever was a hard core at all regarding the division of human races, then it is the division into the three 'races' of Negroids ('blacks'), Mongoloids ('yellows,' Asians) and Caucasians ('whites'), whereby, however, the assignments and sub-assignments, for instance, of Indians, Eskimos, or Australian Aborigines remained and remains completely unclear.

This division actually follows only three external features: skin color, hair coat, and the form of the nose. Additionally it is not thinkable with the simultaneous assignment to the continents of Africa, Asia, Europe, and America.

Race *Bodily feature*	Negroids	Mongoloids	Caucasians
Skin Color	Light to dark brown	Yellowish to reddish/brownish	Light to dark brown
Skin Color – traditional Designation	'black' to 'brown'	'yellow' to 'red'	'white'
Nose	Strong and broad	Low nose root, 'slit eyed'	Narrow and high nose root
Scalp Hair	Curly	Dense and firm	Thin and wavy
Hair Color	Dark	Black	Light to brown
Body Hair	Slight	Slight	Strong

These differences, however, only roughly apply. There are 'Caucasians' who have darker skin color than the lightest 'blacks,' and that indeed after the most disparate divisions by various researchers. As far as skin color is concerned, Asians are *de facto* not able to be differentiated from Europeans, because their spectrum from light to darker corresponds approximately to the spectrum found in Europeans. The 'yellow' skin color of Mongoloids, in contrast, is a pure invention from the end of the 18th century, for which a true justification was never supplied.

According to the classical subdivision, the Ainu of Japan – often also called 'Caucasians' or 'Indo-Europeans' – belong to the 'white' race as do the Drawid of India, the Tamils and Singhalese of Sri Lanka, Persians, Arabs along with Berbers, old Egyptians (Coptics) and Moors, Romani, Teutons and Slavs including Russians and Poles, to name just the most important peoples or families of people. And these people should be so closely related with each other that one can distinguish between Asians ('yellows') and Africans ('blacks')'?

The 1892 Brockhaus Encyclopedia also includes as Caucasians the Hamites along with Berbers, old Egyptians and East Africans, Semites along with Hebrews, Chaldeans, Canaanites, Assyrians, Babylonians, Arabs, and finally the Aryans along with Indians, Medes, Persians, Afghanis, Curds, Armenians, etc. "The black-haired, dark-eyed type, with a skin color including almost all shades up to truly black, also belongs to this group. They include the majority of the inhabitants of Southern Europe, North Africa, Southwest Asia." Could, therefore, by all appearances 'blacks,' really be Caucasians and form one race with Middle Europeans?

Even the leading race researcher of the Third Reich, in his 1982 newly republished and sinister work *The Nordic Race among the Indo-Germanic people of Asia*,[26] counts, among others, the following peoples as Indo-Germanic with a Nordic element: Indians, Scythians, Javanese, Belutshis, Afghanis, Persians, Tajiks, Saks and Armenians.

Furthermore, how much sense does the expression 'colored' make, if the 'white' race itself encompasses an enormous spectrum from light to dark? Is it not just imaginary to say that 'we' are 'white' and the others are 'colored'? Is it not just always haphazardly connected with an implication that allows an assessment to be derived on the basis of color?

It is only known to a few that he speaks of a much greater spectrum of peoples when he speaks of 'blacks' and 'yellows.' 'Black' is quite obviously used for very different peoples, who aside from skin color mostly have nothing to do with each other and whose skin color lightness additionally exhibits a broad spectrum.

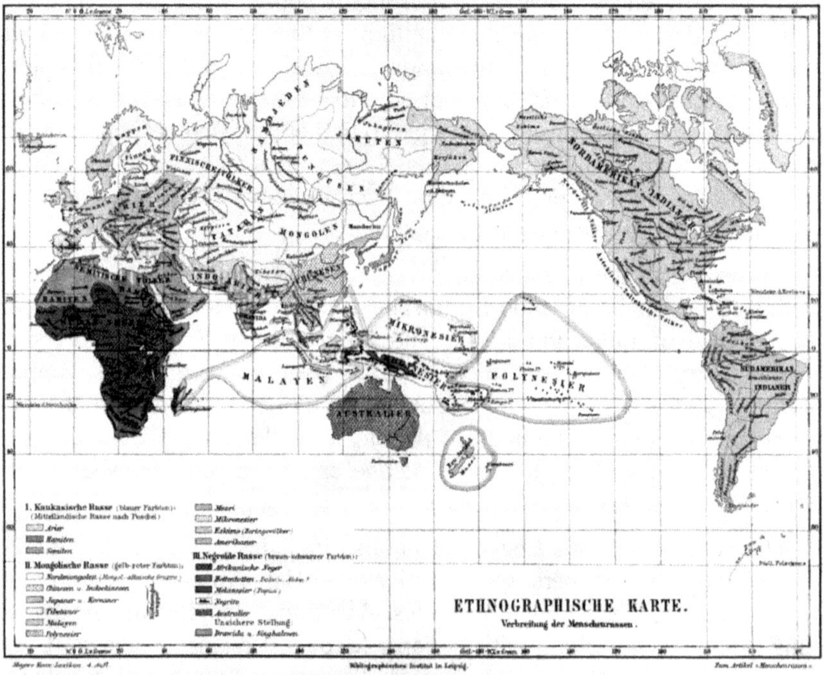

Illustration 1: A traditional map of the races of the 19. century (from the leading German encyclopedia 'Meyers')[27]

---

[26] Hans F. K. Günther/Jürgen Spanuth, *Die nordische Rasse bei den Indogermanen Asiens*, Pähl: Verlag Hohe Warte, 1982.

Why should one classify in this manner at all? When a census is conducted in the USA, information is also collected as to whether a person is white, black, native American, or Hispanic. Apart from the many descendants from mixed marriages and from the fact that many immigrants do not even know themselves precisely who their ancestors were, the latter category shows how senseless this categorization is. This is due to the fact that Hispanics only have a common language, but otherwise originate from completely different countries, peoples, and backgrounds.

The American President Barack Hussein Obama is the offspring of a Kenyan student from the Kenyan Luo and a 'white' American. According to his ancestry, he has nothing to do with most of the 'blacks' in the USA, who are descendants brought over from diverse African tribes many generations ago. But since his skin color is not 'white,' he is viewed as a 'black' politician. Such a classification has no real informational value.

Body Size

Let us take body size as an example, which in all people with little exception lies between 120 and 200 cm. There is a people in the Congo that has the smallest group mean, and that is 142 cm. The highest mean for a people is in the Upper Nile in Sudan, where the value is 185 cm. It is not coincidental that both people groups belong to 'blacks.' The Masai in East Africa are known for their size, which one traces back to the fact that they almost exclusively live off of animal products. Tall Ethiopians, who win at the Olympics, are known around the world. At the same time the fact that the shortest people on earth are Africans was taken as a sign that they lag developmentally. On account of this, there is no question that body height is not suited for racially dividing people, but that changed nothing of the fact that for 150 years one was of the opinion that body height could be so used .

Throughout the centuries, average body height in Central Europe fluctuated significantly, primarily due to living conditions and the availability of food. The low point came in the 17th and 18th centuries, when the average was 163 cm for men. The value today for 18-35 year old German men is 180 cm, and for women the value is 167 cm. Much research has shown that the average body height found in a region is a direct indicator of living conditions.[28] As a result, the population in North Korea since World War II

---

[27] Http://de.wikipedia.org/w/index.php?title=Datei:Meyers_b11_s0476a.jpg&filetime stamp=20100119134424 (07.03.2011)

[28] Marcus Anhäuser, „Wohlstand macht lang", in: *Süddeutsche Zeitung*, February 14, 2006.

has stagnated at an average of 159 cm, and in South Korea, on the other hand, the number has increased to 165 cm. All of this has little to do with 'race.'

Doctrines about Skin Color and how they developed

All attempts to make a true classification of human skin color and to assign skin color to certain ethnicities have to be viewed as unsuccessful efforts. Indeed, the rate of pigmentation that determines skin color, above all the melanin, is genetically conditioned. But it varies within all ethnicities and all the more in greater geographic regions. The lightest Asians are as light as the lightest Europeans, and the darkest 'Caucasians' ('whites') – regardless of which of the many early race divisions one prefers – are as dark as almost all Asians and surely exceed more than half of the Africans in this respect.

By the way: Most researchers assume today that the darker skin tone is the more historic one and that the lighter European and Asian skin tones developed independently of each other.

Historians have shown long ago that doctrines about skin color, in the form they have been commonly known since the time of Carl von Linné (1707-1778), are not based on research or biological reality, but were rather developed to explain alleged cultural superiority.[29]

Walter Demel has examined the initial sources of Europeans traveling to China, who, along with Marco Polo, held the Chinese to be 'white.' It was not until the last third of the 18th century that the Chinese were seen as 'pale yellow' or 'wheaten,' what is ultimately parallel to 'reds' and 'yellows.' This has little to do with any physical realities, but it has a lot to do with European pigeonholing. It is not by accident that the first person who spoke about a 'yellow' race was the philosopher Immanuel Kant, who never left Königsberg and presumably never saw an Asian during his life. Yellow symbolized the Middle Kingdom and emperor of China. But skin does not become yellow just from that, and this also applies to the many Asian peoples such as the Japanese, Koreans or Thais. 'Yellows' are on the whole *de facto* just as light or dark as Europeans. Due to their advanced civilizations one does not want to designate them as 'brown' or 'black,' and they were also not able to be called 'white,' so 'yellow' was a good compromise.

---

[29] The most important historical works on the topic of where teaching on skin color arose are Demel, Chinesen, *Op. cit.*; Hund, *Rassismus: Konstruktion, Op. cit.*, Böckelmann, *Gelben, Op. cit.* (for details see the bibliography).

That 'reds' have their ornamental painting to thank for their symbolized color and not their skin color, has been shown long ago. It is a self serving declaration to say that on the whole the entire Indian genre only used land but neither settled nor occupied it, just because they hunted while freely wandering over the prairie. This was not even the case with the bulk of Indians, but it made it easier for American settlers to take the land from the Indians. This is the basis upon which the highest court in the USA decided that Indians only utilized their land for short periods of time in order to hunt wild animals but never saw the land as their property. Almost all Indians were *de facto* settled and lived in villages, alternating in winter and summer between permanent tent settlements. Additionally, most of them lived from crop farming and not from hunting roaming animals.

Origination of Skin Color Doctrine			
Sequence	*Color*	*Time*	*Prior Designation*
1	'Black' ('Negro')	Prior to the 18th century	'Moors,' Africans
2	'White'	Beginning of the 18th century	
3	'Yellow' ('slit-eyed')	Middle of the 18th century	Chinese, Asians
4	'Red' ('redskin')	Middle of the 18th century	Indians

Excursus: Ethiopians ("People of Cush") in the Old and New Testaments

The Old Testament assumes that all people can and will pray to God. It is a matter of course that African people are also included: "Envoys will come from Egypt; Cush will submit herself to God" (Psalm 68:31); I will record Rahab and Babylon among those who acknowledge me – Philistia too, and Tyre, along with Cush . . ." (Psalm 87:4).

What Luther and others rendered *Mohren,* the Old Testament names 'Cush,' i.e., Nubia (today predominantly in Sudan) or 'Ethiopians.' Conversely, Amos 9:7 clarifies that God treated Israelites, Egyptians, and Ethiopians equally in judgment.

In church history the fact that the first non-Jew to convert to following Jesus Christ was a 'Black' Ethiopian looms large (Acts 8:27-39). He was namely the finance minister of the Ethiopian queen (Acts 8:27). In Ethiopia, in which many 'black' Jews lived (and live), the first Christian kingdom in history soon emerged!

Whether on Pentecost the pilgrims from Egypt and Libya (Acts 2:9-11) were dark skinned or not is not completely clear. However, in church history it is taken to be the case. Among the 16 named native regions, it is indeed hardly likely that there were 'white' pilgrims from Europe.

While not reported in the New Testament itself, it was taken early on as agreed that there were *three* wise men from the orient who were the first to worship Jesus, one of whom was 'black' (who is most often ascribed the name "Caspar"). He is found in practically all representations of Christian art, in which the three wise men (kings) appear before the child in the crib. The depiction of a black person worshipping Christ has made a positive impression on theological thought for a long time.

How do stereotypical Images of Differences and Diversity come into Existence?

Criteria, on the basis of which races are defined, can be arbitrarily chosen. A member of the public decides today who belongs to a 'race' based on criteria the individual himself lays down or owing to criteria he or she finds prescribed by education, the media, or the political realm, independent of any scientific criteria.[30]

For instance, why is it that we sense that Chinese or Ukrainians look so different? The appearance of a person is not only determined by biological circumstances, but rather also from that individual's culture, i.e., the entirety of what is learned and accepted from one's environment. From the time we are small we learn and mimic gestures, a way of walking, and the language of our environment. Hair styles, make-up, and clothing go one step further. From the time we are small we also learn to differentiate between the faces and people in our environment.

If we suddenly meet people who do not fit into our schema, they appear to us to be completely different. Furthermore, if we meet several people from a people group that is unknown to us, they, surprisingly, appear to us

---

[30] According to, for instance, Katrin Monen, *Das Verbot der Diskriminierung: Eine Untersuchung aufgrund der Rasse, des Geschlechts und der sexuellen Identität im deutschen und U.S.-amerikanischen Privatrecht* (Dissertation), Baden-Baden: Nomos, 2008, p. 91.

to all be the same or similar. As Germans we have never learned to differentiate between Japanese, although Japanese, among themselves, are naturally as different as Germans. Should the occasion arise, we would not be able to give the police a precise description. Rather, we would only be able to say: "He somehow looked like an Asian." If we were to live a long time in Japan, we would be able to differentiate between people there and describe them.

I have a good friend who is 'black' and who grew up in Switzerland. His parents had good career positions in Switzerland. He speaks Swiss German, behaves like a Swiss German, and looks like one, too – except for his skin color. In the twilight every Swiss takes him to be a Swiss, because he moves 'correctly,' etc., and on the telephone sounds in any case Swiss. It is only in the light that a certain bewilderment arises.

At certain times in the Islamic world it was Arabs, Persians, and Turks who were respectively the ruling 'people,' and as a result they are until the present hostile towards each other. Which European can even assign people from the three Islamic groups, Arabs, Persians, and Turks to one people group if they are groomed and dressed the same? The threatening appearance that many Europeans sense when they see oriental people is only experienced when such people have certain typical features, for example a strong, dark beard. Less conspicuously dressed, groomed and without hearing the language, a European cannot say whether the person before him is a dark Italian or an Arab from Afghanistan.

Dehumanization and Cannibalism

The 'dehumanization' of other 'races' and groups is also found in the repertoire of racism. Hitler was not the first to declare others – in his case the Jews – to be bacteria, fungus, ape-like and closer to animals than to people. Via numerous depictions, attempts were made to show that Jews resembled apes. This was an approach that had been tried most intensively on 'Negros' for centuries.[31] Typically no one made reference to the fact that 'whites' have thin lips in common with chimpanzees . . .

---

[31] Regarding the history see Gould, *Mensch*, pp. 118-156.

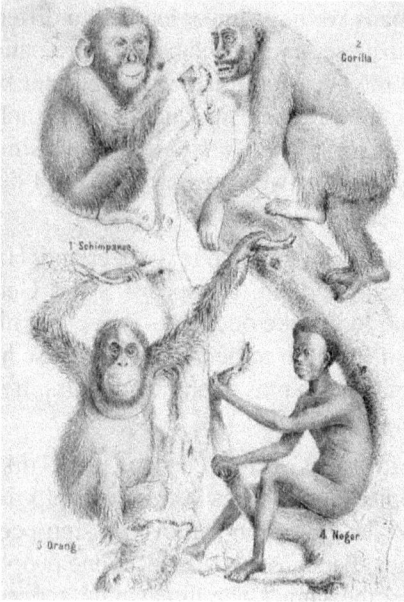

Illustration 2: A book by Ernst Haeckel (1877) compares apes and 'negroes'[32]

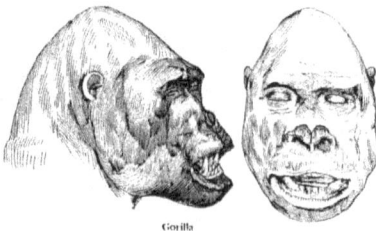

Illustration 3: With gimmicks like this the 19th century tried to prove similarities between apes and Africans (from the academic book 'Types of Mankind', 1845)[33]

[32] Ernst Haeckel, *Anthropogenie oder Entwicklungsgeschichte des Menschen.* Leipzig: Verlag von Wilhelm Engelmann, 1877, dritte, umgearbeitete Auflage. Tafel XIV. after p. 516.

[33] Quoted by Sandra Harding (Ed.), *The "Racial" Economy of Science: Toward a Democratic Future.* Bloomington (IN): Indiana University Press, 1993. p. 88.

For centuries Japanese considered Europeans to be barbarian and animal-like, because in their opinion they had so much hair and had so much to do with dogs. The Chinese thought that Europeans were close to apes and considered them albinos, who through some unnatural way or through demons had lost their color. The way Europeans sweated made them threatening. Frank Böckelmann[34] has exhaustively shown how Japanese, Chinese, and West Africans viewed Europeans, but also how Asians saw 'blacks,' for instance. Insofar as racist disdain is concerned, no one is really behind anyone else. These points of view are to us preposterous and without any merit, but the European viewpoint was no less groundless.

In a study I conducted on 'cannibalism,'[35] I reported in detail on the ethnological discussion as to whether cannibalism had ever been part of a culture or whether the New York anthropology professor William Arens is correct with his thesis that there is no such evidence about any nation that would ever hold up in court.[36] Even among researchers who hold this position to be excessive, it is beyond question that in the far majority of cases of cannibalism which have been reported throughout history, they have been without witnesses and only a fraction of the reports were and are able to be verified. It is rather the case that 'cannibalism' is a favorite allegation against strangers that regularly served Europeans well in justifying the exploitation of Indians or Africans. The first Christians were likewise suspected of cannibalism by the Romans as were the Irish by the Greek historian Strabon or the Scythians by his predecessor Herodotus.

David Livingstone, anthropologist, researcher on Africa, and distinguished missionary came to a similar result regarding Africa in 1874. He traveled through large parts of Africa, among other locations, on a search for evidence of cannibalism. He was astonished to find that there were no pieces of evidence. However, he did ascertain that almost all blacks were convinced that whites were man-eaters, which was an accusation that the first explorers of the Gambia River had to address as early as 1455.

---

[34] Böckelmann, *Gelben, Op. cit.*

[35] "Cannibalism and Human Sacrifice Vindicated?" *Christianity and Society* 10 (2000) 1: 11-17 + 2: 4-9, Download from www.kuyper.org/main/uploads/ volume_10_no_1.pdf and www.kuyper.org/main/uploads/volume_10_no_2.pdf; see also as MBS Text 91 under http://www.bucer.eu/uploads/media/mbstexte 091_a.pdf.

[36] William Arens, *The Man-Eating Myth: Anthropology and Anthropophagy*, New York: Oxford University Press, 1979.

4. IQ Racism

Are 'Whites' more intelligent than 'Blacks'?

Since in the meantime all attempts to differentiate among races according to some type of measurement have failed, a newer, allegedly exact measurement method to differentiate between the races became popular. This is the series test used to measure intelligent quotients (IQ). "What craniometry (the measurement of the cranium) was for the 19th century, intelligence tests have become for the 20th century . . ."[37] The IQ appears to be the last remaining reserve of those who are of the opinion that the 'white race' (if not Europeans alone) is superior. Why was it not the Japanese or the Jews (who, however, are 'whites') who colonized the world – as their average IQ on the basis of the same investigations in the USA are higher? And why have Europeans or Americans not offered the Japanese and the Jews global sovereignty but rather are hostile to them?

The Bell Curve is a controversially-discussed work by two Harvard professors, Charles Murray and Richard Herrnstein, and represents above all the thesis that black Americans achieve IQ test results that are on average about 15 points lower than whites. They maintain that this difference is at least 60% genetically conditioned and for this reason IQ cannot be raised through education. The following can be said about this:

1.   Supposing that the results are beyond critique, the answer to the question of how the differences are explained (genetically, 'racially' or, in fact, through social and cultural conditions) is as open as it has always been. This is due to the fact that because researchers are not able to prove there is an intelligence gene. Should the fact that in the USA 40% of all 'blacks,' but only 5% of 'white' children live in poverty play no role?

2.   Whether the members of the various skin color groups would differ from each other in terms of IQ if they grew up under almost the same social conditions has not been investigated. Some other studies tell a different story. For instance, middle class Canadian black Africans score 20 points higher on IQ tests than other participants with the same African ancestry.

3.   What is addressed is an overall average. With all groups there is an entire distribution all the way up to the extremely gifted. Methods re-

---

[37]   Gould, *Mensch, Op. cit.*, p. 20; very good on this issue is Dave Unander, *Shattering the Myth of Race: Genetic Realities and Biblical Truths*, Valley Forge: Judson Press, 2000, p. 82ff.

lating to averages are very unreliable, due to the fact that with all groups the same range is found.

Are the measurements themselves reliable?

For numerous reasons they cannot be:

1. There are no culture-free IQ tests. If a German is asked what is important for Eskimo children, Germans stand there dumbfounded and vice versa. American IQ tests reflect a western understanding of education, not, however, a universal understanding of intelligence or knowledge.

2. Higher gifting or high gifting is known to not be a guarantee for success and superiority. Most highly gifted people fail in everyday life if family or mentors are not in the background. In addition to the things an IQ test measures are various forms of intelligence that are important, for instance so-called EQ, or emotional intelligence, the ability to communicate with others, the ability to work out problems, and the ability to adapt to the environment.

3. Not least of all, the limitation of the investigation to 'blacks' and 'whites' is wrong, due to the fact that there are, as mentioned already, ethnicities which on average perform better on IQ tests than 'white' Americans or Europeans. This is namely the case with Jews and Japanese, whose results are 11 points higher.

Primitive Languages?

Regarding the topic of IQ, there is something to add: A portion of the IQ measurement has to do with language abilities. In earlier times it was thought in all seriousness that 'primitive' peoples had 'primitive' languages. The evolutionary theory of cultural development from a primitive people to a civilized people suggests this. We have known for a long time that this is nonsense. Primitive peoples often have highly complex and strongly differentiated languages. There is actually no such thing as a primitive language. Rather, there are at most languages which others can learn with more ease (e.g., English) or with more difficulty (e.g., Japanese).

"Modern linguistics has gone even further: every language, every dialect, has an equally complex structure. Noam Chomsky concerned himself with the ability of people to independently work through the complicated rules of their mother tongue and to build running sentences which the individual has never heard before. Present day linguists are in agreement that every small child could learn any language, independent of which language the child's parents speak. This also makes plain what linguistics can and cannot achieve when it studies our early history. Relatedness between languages can help reconstruct migrations of people, but it can never erect a ranking between peoples."[38] Every baby in the world is so unbelievably intelligent that it can decipher and learn every human language.

European cultural Development?

Farming was not invented in Europe, and for millennia European superiority was not expected. Even the Roman Empire, the center of which was after all in Rome, was not considered to be European. Its longest surviving piece, the Byzantine Empire, existed into the 15th century in part in Asia and even in Africa. European superiority did not develop until the 15th century and above all via the superiority in weapons technology. At around 1000 A.D. no one would have had a reason to suppose that Europeans would determine the direction of world history over a period of some 600 years. What, however, does 600 years mean in terms of genetic or biological developments? It is indeed justified to ask about the causes of the ascendancy of Europeans. Was is the good climate, the way of life and nutrition, the Christian religion, the competition that arose through the diversity of political entities, or the increased immunity against epidemics after tremendous losses due to them, which Indians in America did not experience? All theories put forward by historians were supposedly, as is so often the case, in some way or another simultaneously correct. The only thing is, they have nothing to do with the question of race or any sort of biological determination or superiority of Europeans.

5. We are all 'MixedBreeds'

'Mestizos' and 'Bastards'?

Christian Schüller and Petrus van der Let appropriately call their book *The Human Race: We're All a Mixed Breed*. The "results of genetics," according to the authors, "tell the story of people in a completely new way: It is a story of continual commingling. The more precisely we analyze a people group, the more diverse it becomes. Exceptions are the rule!"[39]

One of the most peculiar phenomena in almost all cultures is how negatively 'racial mixing' is viewed, while year for year millions of men and women fall in love regardless of 'racial borders,' marry and have children,

---

[38]   Christian Schüller/Petrus van der Let, *Rasse Mensch: Jeder Mensch ein Mischling (The Human Race: We're all a Mixed Breed)*, Aschaffenburg: Alibri, 1999, pp.27-28.

[39]   Schüler and van der Let, p. 23.

and leave no one to define the borders of race. Biologically speaking there is nothing that speaks against it, and if biology is to play some sort of role, we know that an alien gene pool is always better than frequent 'inbreeding.'

'Bastard' is not only a curse word with reference to an origin that occurs out of wedlock but also has the meaning of "an animal or plant emerging by a crossing of race or species," or as a dog without a genealogy, it is up to the present, all too willingly conferred upon people. Why then do European languages only have derogatory terms and no neutral words for children born as a result of bi-national relationships?

Along with the warning about 'racial mixing' apparently comes the fact that opinions of where one's own, admissible race begins and ends varies greatly and is arbitrarily chosen. May a German marry someone who is French? It was not too long ago that such an occurrence was viewed as a racial problem. Today that is no longer the case, provided that it is a 'real' French person and not a dark-skinned immigrant . . .

Mind you, this should not be treated as if every warning about 'bi-national' marriages is amiss. Whoever chooses a partner with another language and from another cultural environment, just as someone who chooses a partner from another class in society, has numerous problems to overcome. Differences in language can make marital communication more difficult, and various expectations on the part of parents-in-law can make life arduous. A modern, atheistic, German woman would have a difficult time living with a prince from the royal house of Saudi Arabia. However, all of this is neither biologically nor racially based. Rather, it lies in the different language, culture, religion, education, and societal class of the people involved.

What are the actual problems that 'Mestizos' (Indians and whites), mulattos (blacks and whites), and Zambos (Indians and blacks) have in Latin America, where they often account for the majority of the population? Are they not viewed as 'mixed breeds' because we have three races in mind according to skin color, when in actual fact *we* are just as much 'mixed breeds'? And which German even knows whether among his ancestors there might not be Africans and Asians – this is something that genetic research suggests as a conclusion to each one of us!

Looked at mathematically, every German at Luther's time 20 generations ago had 1 million ancestors, which is to say theoretically more people than lived in Germany at that time. Since nephews and cousins married and through other kinships of our ancestors, the number is naturally reduced. But who is to say where all these ancestors came from? With 30 genera-

tions we are already at 1 billion ancestors, and with 40 generations back –
for instance in the year 1000 A.D. – at theoretically 1 trillion ancestors,
that is to say, a multiple of the number of all people who have ever lived.
The idea that the majority of our ancestors come from a small region and
not from all parts of the world is in the best case wishful thinking. Who
wants to guarantee the there are no Mongoloids among his ancestors from
the time when 'streams of Huns' made it all the way to France around 450
A.D.?

Out of the more than 35 million Hispanics who were counted in the 2000
census in the USA, 42.2% described themselves as belonging to 'another
race,' 47.9% classified themselves as white Hispanics. 6.3% of Hispanics
classified themselves as stemming from other races. In actuality there is
naturally no race of Hispanics in the USA – they are a motley group from
all parts of the world, who not only have English but a variation of Spanish
as a mother tongue. Classifying people this way is something that arises in
the heads of individuals.

Percentage of 'Mestizos' in Latin America	Percentage of Mulattos ('White' and 'Black') in selected Countries
Costa Rica 94% (Europeans and Mestizo)	Dominican Republic 73%
El Salvador 90%	Puerto Rico 30%
Honduras 90%	Suriname 30%
Venezuela 75-80% (Mestizos and Mulattos)	Colombia 14%
Panama 70%	Venezuela 10%
Chile 65%	Jamaica 7%
Nicaragua 69%	Haiti 5%
Ecuador 65%	
Mexico 60%	
Colombia 58% (+14% Mulattos)	
Belize 49%	
Peru 37%	
Bolivia 30%	
Argentina 13%	
Uruguay 8%	

The total percentage of those designated 'Pardos,' a mixed population in
Brazil, amounts to 38%, and Mulattos and Caboclos (Indian and European
mixed breeds) belong to this group, as do other mixed breeds. In Brazil
there was a broad political stream of *branqueamento*. The intention was to

improve the 'Brazilian race' and via an admixture of 'white blooded' European immigrants cause the 'black element' in the Brazilian population to disappear. This measure was often taken by dark-skinned Brazilians who themselves tried to shake off the alleged disgrace for their offspring.

Commingling of People throughout History

The myth of 'pure blood' not mixed with foreign races over the millennia, cannot be supported by the evidence. Nevertheless, the idea simply does not die. The right wing extremist party NPD (National Democratic Party of Germany), for example, defines race as follows: 'A race is a society of people who through separation from other people over a long enough period of time have developed differently than the other people of the species and who have achieved genetic homogeneity and approximate genetic consistency.'[40]

Making such a statement with respect to people refutes the term race. Where has there ever been such a separation? Humanity has a history of migrations, war campaigns, trade relationships that span the globe, and even in the case of small people groups which actually have been separated for a long period of time, Bushmen or Australian Aborigines, for example, no one knows how their early history looked. Furthermore, genetics has taught us that in the past these people also migrated over great distances. In the NDP (National Democratic Party of Germany) Publishing House, Johannes P. Ney is trying to lay out a new doctrine of race, but he himself writes that there are not 'pure' human races. He also doubts that isolated Polynesians possess 'pure blood,' since as maritime masters they surely traveled extensively in the South Seas and liberally mixed with other peoples of the South Seas.[41]

Undiluted Germanic People or Turks?

The smaller ethnic groups are in comparison to alleged 'major races,' the more senseless it is to assume there are racial differences that were kept free of all types of 'intermixture.'

For instance, most Turks believe in a 'Turkish race.' Actually, however, as a point of intersection between Europe and Asia in the multiethnic state of the Byzantine Empire, as well as in the multiethnic state of the Ottoman Empire in what is now the soil of present day Turkey, countless people and groups have mixed with each other for thousands of years. That the father

---

[40] Johannes P. Ney, *Reizwort Rasse*, Riesa: Deutsche Stimme Verlag, 2000, p. 20.

[41] Ney, p. 41.

of modern Turkey and of Turkish nationalism, Mustafa Kemal Atatürk, was himself of Albanian ancestry illustrates this fact well.

It has been attempted for a long time to view Germans and French as racially different and, for instance, to go back to Germanic people and Celts in conducting this exercise. Charles the Great is held to be the progenitor of the French king as well as the progenitor of the German emperor, and at Charles' time Franks and Germans were even able to communicate with each other by language. The first known dual language document is the agreement to split the empire among Charles' sons. Germany and France continually moved their borders back and forth, the French king had feudal possession in Germany and at times also wanted to be German emperor. For hundreds of years French was the language of education in Germany. In Switzerland and in the Alsace including Strasbourg, the two cultural groups became blurred. In spite of this, there are individual Germans who still imagine that there is genetically something such as a German and a Frenchman, and that the differences between both countries are racially based and not a question of their different languages, culture, history, world view, form of government, and legal system.

My ancestors are, for example, probably Reformed Huguenots who, after having been driven out of France, lived temporarily as 'Salzburg Protestants' in Austria. Thereafter, they migrated on to Gdansk and there reclaimed land in parts of Prussia. Who knows who would show up if I looked back twenty generations into my ancestry? Am I a German or a Frenchman?

If anyone in Central Europe wants to speak of some sort of race that is in any way stable after all the 'racial mixing' that took place in the Roman Empire, subsequent migrations, campaigns of conquest from every direction, the invasion of Asian troops on horseback, and immigration from all over the world, then the only explanation is that the wish is father to the thought and the modern nation state would like to have a biological, religious, or other type of fixed anchoring for its citizens. Studies of Y-chromosomes suggest that the people of Europe have no identifiable origin but that they all go back to repeatedly new waves of immigration from all different directions.

I wrote my first dissertation on Theodor Christlieb, who was by birth a Württembergian and primarily active in Bonn as a theologian in the 19th century. He has the following circumstances to thank for his name, namely that his grandfather was a Turkish foundling baptized "Christlieb" by Württembergian foster parents. He held himself for a stalwart German.

Kaiser Wilhelm II did as well, for he called him to be court chaplain. Christlieb was albeit unable to take on the post due to his death.

Again it is genetic research, with it very latest results, that comes to our aid: "Only a few Germans are truly Germanic: Only about six percent of all Germans have Germanic origin on their father's side. This is what is maintained by a study from a genetics laboratory. According to the study, 30% stem from Eastern Europe. And there was some additional information that came out as a result of this: German women are more German than men. Every one out of ten Germans has, according to a Swiss study, Jewish ancestors . . . Researchers additionally [found] out . . . that only six percent of all Germans had Germanic origins from the father's side. According to the study, 30% stem from Eastern Europe. For the study, which has been unpublished up to now, 19,457 genetic analyses were compared. Moreover, in the course of their investigations of maternal lines, the genetic researchers came to the conclusion that German women are more often of Germanic ancestry than German men, namely 50% of them. Researchers explain this difference as due to the shorter lifetimes of masculine forefathers. Modern genetics show the senselessness of racism, says Imm Pazos, who is one of the scientists associated with the study. All genetic analyses demonstrated that every person has countless roots and in every person there is a 'mishmash.'"[42]

I make no pretence of the fact that I am admittedly a non-scientist who is somewhat concerned about whether science, in the case of genetic research, has bitten off more than it can chew. It could be that much of what is maintained today will be adjusted by the next generation of genetic researchers. However, even if that were to be the case, none of it would presumably provide a meaningful basis for a return to racist thinking.

Excursus: Was the Old Testament Prohibition against Marriage to Non-Jews racist?

The Old Testament often reports on divorce from unbelieving, pagan women (e.g., Ezra 9:1-10, 44, in particular Ezra 9:1 and Ezra 10:3; Nehemiah 9:2; 10:29; 13:3; Malachi 2:10-16). The prohibition against marrying non-Jewish partners was, however, not a racial but rather a religious prohibition. What was prohibited was "marrying the daughter of a foreign god" (Malachi 2:11b), that is to say, a woman who believes in another god. If a heathen, either male or female, converted to the God of Israel, they were

---

[42] www.welt.de/wissenschaft/article1398825/Nur_wenige_Deutsche_sind_echte_ Germanen.html (Article dated November 25, 2007).

indeed able to be married, just as vice versa one was not allowed to marry a Jewish male or female who served foreign gods. In Jesus' genealogy (Matthew 1:1-17) Matthew four times mentions women, and indeed each time it has to do with a heathen woman: Tamar, Bathsheba, Rahab, and Ruth. Ruth was by nature a Moabite (Ruth 1:4) and that, although the Moabites were specifically excluded from God's people (Deuteronomy 23:4). However, because she swore to her mother-in-law: "Your people will be my people and your God my God" and with that converted to the Jewish faith, she was able to be taken as a wife by Boaz and become the most well known matriarch of David and Jesus.

II. On the History of Racism and its Justification

1. The History of Racist Theories

Antiquity

It is a matter of dispute whether there was racism in antiquity or not. Some argue that there was neither anything corresponding to the term 'race' nor was there anything that was likened to the later contempt for 'blacks.' Antiquity was enormously multicultural, and the idea of "one people, one nation, one state," that is to say, the nation state, was completely unknown in antiquity. Even slavery followed ethnicity less than being proof of the fact that class differences were an understood part of all societies of antiquity.

As a start there was, however, racism in other regions of the world. The Chinese disdained all people who did not belong to the 'middle.' Also, the Indian caste system can be categorized as racism, as I will expound further below.

The Middle Ages and the Enlightenment tied in with the Greek philosopher Aristotle, who taught that 'barbarians' were by nature inferior and for that reason born for slavery. One had to deal with them as with animals. Even if what Aristotle meant by 'nature' (*physis*) was raison d'être and not biology as was later the case, what is found here is the connection between a biological-bodily group membership with features of incapacity for civilization and a resemblance to animals that justified, yes, even obliged them to, enslavement.

The Emergence of European Racism in the 15th Century

With the Christian doctrine of universal human dignity, "a new concept that had been foreign from antiquity up to that time"[43] appeared in world history. In the narrower sense, the actual history of European racism only began in the 15th century, after almost a millennium of Christian history.

It could actually be said that prior to 1400 there were no ideologically defined 'races,'[44] if it is true that Arabian slave traders did not develop their view of the inferiority of black slaves at an earlier time. In any event, beginning in 1400 Spaniards and Portuguese, through their business rela-

---

[43] Christian Geulen, *Geschichte des Rassismus*, München: C.H. Beck 2007, p. 38.

[44] According to, in part, Unander, *Shattering*, p. 5.

tionships, not only brought the Arabian slave trade to Europe but also, with the slave trade, the idea also came that black Africans were either not human or less than human[45] and could not even be converted to Christianity. In addition there was the Islamic point of view that Noah, in Ham, had cursed the black race.[46].

At the end of the 15th century and beginning of the 16th century, as a consequence of the *Reconquista*, which was the Christian recapture of all of Spain, a new point of view established itself in Spain. To be sure most Jews and remaining Muslim Moors had been forced to be baptized from 1492 onwards, but now what had been a common religious intolerance had become a racial intolerance. On the basis of their ancestry, Jews and Moors also remained unbelievers and enemies after baptism.

Therefore, alongside the Spanish politics of 'blood purity' (*limpieza de sangre*), Anti-Semitism also took on a new form. It was the Jews who had converted to Christianity or their offspring (Marranos) who became the target, since their religious confession was mistrusted. Whoever had only one grandparent of Jewish descent was not considered 'pure blooded' and was considered dangerous.

A group with common roots is what develops out of a believing Christian community. Actually, everyone who is baptized becomes a part of it. What became of it, however, was a community of heredity, into which a person was born. It was not able to be reached from without, and that is a perversion of the New Testament message.

It is paradoxical that this racism emerged in Spain and Portugal, because simultaneously in the new colonies in Latin America and Middle America the mixing of 'races' was normal. Beginning in 1500 Spaniards wrestled with the question of their relationship to Indians in Latin America. In 1550 the Dominicans Francisco de Vitoria (1492-1549) and Bartolomé de las Casas were able to come out on top in the so-called Valladolid debate as advocates for the Indians against Juan Ginès de Sepúlveda. Indians were thus seen, according to royal and papal law, as people with rights who could convert. Las Casas wrote: "All the races of the world are men, and the definition of all men, and of each of them, is only one, and that is reason."[47] Reality looks different. Beginning in 1510, Aristotle's idea that the

---

[45] Comp. the extensive analyses by Bernard Lewis, *Race and Slavery in the Middle East*, Oxford: Oxford University Press, 1990.

[46] Regarding Ham's curse (Genesis 9:20-27), it can additionally be said that the three sons do not fit into the traditional human racial trichotomy.

[47] Quoted in Fredrickson, *Racism*, p. 37.

enslavement of barbarians was due to their more base human nature was increasingly transferred to 'blacks.'[48] As long as Indians and 'Negros' were able to convert, they were protected by the Christian understanding. Therefore, what began to happen on a grand scale was to report on human sacrifice and cannibalism – and today we know that these reports were largely unjustly made – so that the oppressed people could either be portrayed as *unable to convert* and irreversibly bad or portrayed as *beastly* and inhuman.

All of this helped 'blacks' very little, because of all things Las Casas despised them deeply. Provided that the corresponding passages truly came from him, they gave birth to the idea that in order to protect the Indians, black Africans were to be sent as slave substitutes to the colonies.

The Word 'Race'

The word 'race' reflects the development towards racism from the 14th to the 19th century. The German word 'race' comes from the Romance languages, where *raza* (Spanish), *raça* (Portuguese), *razza* (Italian) und *race* (French) have been used since the 13th century. In German *race* was used for centuries. It was not until the 19th century that the word was Germanized to *Rasse*.

The word was originally used to designate the ancestral lines of aristocrats, that is to say, people of 'noble' or 'blue blood,' in addition to bred races in horse breeding.

Regarding the 'noble blood' of aristocrats, the following can be said in passing: I hold the idea of biological races of humans to be a myth, just as it was in the case of 'nobility.' Even if millions allow themselves to be ruled, because they view aristocrats as hereditarily conditioned for something better, it really has to do with nothing other than a fictitious, if successful, ideology to defend a certain social order. The higher nobility is *de facto* neither automatically bestowed with intelligence nor leadership charisma, nor with health or an understanding of the principles of justice. Rather, it is only a question of one's own feeling of superiority . . .

Racism in the Enlightenment

"Practices of discrimination against minority groups have a long tradition. Up until within the 17th century such exclusionary actions were primarily religiously based. In the course of the 18th and 19th centuries, theo-

---

[48] Comp. Lewis Hanke, *Aristotle and the American Indians*, Chicago: Regnery, 1959.

ries and ideologies came along that people used to classify and hierarchically organize people into biological groups ('races') on the basis of physical, ethnic or cultural features with genetically inheritable characteristics. These ideas served as a basis for justifying colonialism and imperialism as well as domestic actions and discrimination designed to promote the preservation of social and economic privileges."[49]

It was 200 years later, precisely at the time of the explosion of knowledge and of the 'Enlightenment,' that racism was brought into a new phase. "The scientific thought of the Enlightenment was a precondition for the growth of a modern racism based on physical typology."[50] It was this that allowed the Christian 'brake,' that all people are in equal measure the posterity of Adam and images of God, to finally be dissolved. "What made the concept of race so fascinating for philosophers such as Voltaire or Kant, as well as for those who were interested in natural history in the narrower sense, ... was the promise of a natural order, which meant above all describing and organizing the world in a manner that was independent of the teachings of the church and of the people of the church."[51]

According to George M. Fredrickson, "one can easily portray Voltaire as the first thoroughgoing modern racist."[52] The French philosopher actually wanted to criticize Christianity when he questioned the common origin of all human races, but his derogatory statement about black Africans or Jews, for instance, went in a completely different direction, and that, although Voltaire rejected slavery. Even as the Enlightenment fought against slavery and set Jewish emancipation in gear, it continued to expand racial thought and with it justified the most wicked form of contempt for 'Negroes,' comparing them with apes.

The Enlightenment developed the model of historical progress from the nomadic life as hunter-gatherers via the stage as herdsmen and farmers all the way up to civil society, which provided the precondition for social Darwinism. In this way the 'gypsies' per se were primitive, because they had been vagrant people traveling around in covered wagons for centuries.

---

[49] „Nicht ‚Rassen' schaffen Rassismus, sondern Rassismus schafft ‚Rassen'", http://www.ekr-cfr.ch/themen/00023/index.html?lang=de.

[50] Fredrickson, *Racism*, p. 56, see also „Der Rassismus der Aufklärung", in: Christian Delacampagne, *Die Geschichte des Rassismus*, Düsseldorf: Artemis & Winkler, 2005, pp. 125-158, Voltaire pp. 138-139 and Andrew Valls (ed.), *Race and Racism in Modern Philosophy*, Ithaca: Cornell University Press, 2005.

[51] Geulen, *Geschichte*, p. 56.

[52] Fredrickson, *Racism*, p. 62.

The first person who attempted to make a scientific classification of the human race in modern times was Carl von Linné (1707-1778). He was the founder of modern biological taxonomy and had been strongly influenced by Aristotle. In 1766, within the framework of his groundbreaking subdivision of the entire plant and animal world, he placed humans ('Tagmenschen') within four species, named according to four ostensible colors of their skin (*Americanus rufus* = red American, *Europaeus albus* = white European, *Asiaticus luridus* = pale yellow Asian, *Africanus niger* = black African) and their alleged temperaments going back to Greek antiquity.

"Whatever it was that Linné, Blumenbach and other ethnologists had in mind, they were in any case the pioneers of a secular or 'scientific' racism."[53] "Through the evaluation of phenotypic characteristics on the basis of aesthetic criteria, as well as through the combination with intellectual, temperamental and cultural abilities, the race typology that had been worked out in the 18th century prepared the soil for the completely unfurled biological racism of the 19th and 20th centuries."[54]

Joseph Arthur Comte de Gobineau (1816-1882) is considered the inventor of the idea of the Aryan master race and founder of modern 'racial doctrine,' which prepared the way for the worst racism in history. It is interesting that one of the earliest uses of the term *race* came in the 15th century with reference to nobility, since Gobineau explained the demise of his status of nobility with reference to racist degeneration that came about by racial mixing. He prophesied that mixing blood from different races would lead to the extinction of humanity and, thereby, influenced the oft unexpressed negative feelings associated with 'racial mixing.'

Evolutionary Theory and Social Darwinism

What is meant by social Darwinism is the use of evolutionary theory to understand human society and its development as a result of the 'fight for survival.' Franz Stuhlhofer has shown that the use of evolutionary principles such as the fight for survival and the survival of the fittest has been appallingly taken by Charles Darwin himself and applied to humans and peoples.[55] The classic representatives of evolution, such as Herbert Spencer, Edward Tylor, and Lewis Henry Morgan, assumed that human societies, just as biological species, are subject to development processes,

---

[53] Fredrickson, p. 58.

[54] Léon Poliakov/Christian Delacampagne/Patrick Girard, *Rassismus: Über Fremdenfeindlichkeit und Rassenwahn*, Hamburg: Luchterhand, 1992, pp.20-21.

[55] Franz Stuhlhofer, *Charles Darwin*, Berneck: Schwengeler 1988, pp. 37-42 and pp. 136-137.

in which success and survival of those best suited lead to permanent improvement in the group.

"If it were amiss to say that there is a direct path from social Darwinism to the Third Reich and its practices based on heredity and race, then it is still the case that the 'direction and ideation' that took on a specifically channeled life form in the National Socialistic state was inspired by social Darwinism. When Hitler proclaimed in *Mein Kampf* that there is no special status assigned to humanity, one has to 'understand and grasp the fundamental imperative of the workings of nature' to which humanity is also subject, he drew on the biological-monistic worldview that had long before him become the credo of social Darwinists."[56]

It actually appeared to be the case that evolutionary theory, which did away with mankind's special position in the natural world, provided a good explanation for the development of cultures and the differences one finds between people groups. And it all appeared to be scientifically based. It appears, too, that it is always good if science receives an ethical requirement and is testable and able to be critically analyzed outside of science. "Scientific racism of the explicitly or implicitly polygenetic kind did not take hold in England until after the mid-nineteenth century, mainly because of the strength of evangelical Christianity and its commitment to the belief that all human beings descended from Adam. ... In France ethnological discussion was uninhibited by Protestant Evangelicalism and could take a more radical turn than in Britain or even the United States."[57]

In the meantime evolutionary researchers have themselves corrected many of the errors that led them straight into racism, and in so doing have returned to some once derided points of view, such as, for instance, that all people have a common ancestry. But over against all appeals to modern scientific research results, we should retain a certain healthy skepticism regarding scientific results that are presented as if they were absolute final conclusions.

Colonialism

Any book about racism should actually include a history of colonialism, which, however, is not possible to present in a short and compact manner. Racism, according to many historians,[58] was admittedly not the decisive

---

[56]   Kurt Nowak, „Euthanasie und Sterilisierung im Dritten Reich", Göttingen: Vandenhoeck und Ruprecht, 1978, p. 25.

[57]   Fredrickson, *Racism*, pp. 66-67.

[58]   Fredrickson, p. 110 and the authors named there.

ideology found everywhere among all colonial rulers. Often it only provided a retroactive justification, for instance to the homeland's inhabitants. Additionally, colonialism was also strongly influenced by competition and war that existed between Europeans. In this connection one thinks of the Boers and British in South Africa, who did not balk at exploiting 'whites.'

'Colonial Times' are designated as a modern epoch, based on the colonialism emanating from European powers, and that commenced at the beginning of the 15th century. It's petering out was touched off by the end of World War II, such that from 1946 to 1965 almost all earlier colonies became independent. Next to this there were, naturally, colonial times and colonial powers, such as the Roman, the Ottoman, the Chinese, or the Soviet empire, that throughout all times and on all continents were connected with the subjugation of many people.

Furthermore, with the term 'imperialism' one designates, if you will, the collecting of colonies, i.e., an orientation in national politics that seeks the domination of as many regions and peoples as possible within the framework of a global struggle for power. With this, then, comes a global and political influence that extends well beyond one's original dominion.

Slavery

While African peoples had enslaved each other for a long time, and while Arab princes finally became the lords of the African slave trade, the European entanglement began in 1444 when a Portuguese expedition in Lagos unloaded 235 slaves from Mauritania. In 1510, the first 50 black Africans were brought from Spain to Haiti to work in the silver mines, and in 1619 the first slaves arrived on the soil of what is today the United States of America.

The transatlantic slave trade was born, [59] which was a business triangle in which cheap goods, hard liquor, and weapons from Europe, through the inclusion of Arab slave traders, were often exchanged for slaves, and these slaves were then exchanged for American colonial goods. With this it was taken for granted that there would be a social and physical death of a portion of the slaves, since slaves were valued and treated as goods. Between 1450 and 1900 it is estimated that 11.7 million slaves from Africa were carried off to America. Of this total, 9.8 million actually found America to be their country of destination. Between 1 and 2 million slaves died during approximately 50,000 passages.

---

[59] Comp., in part., Delacampagne, *Geschichte*, pp. 112-124.

Excursus: Evangelicals and Slavery

In addition to other economic and social factors, Evangelical revivalism was significantly involved in bringing an end to slavery. It is at this point that the designation *Evangelicals* came about in the first place. This applies to the legal abolishment of slavery in Great Britain as well as to the anti-slavery movement in the USA.[60]

It was in 1688 that Quakers in England and the USA first demanded that all slaves be released. By 1780 all Quakers had released their slaves. George Whitefield und John Wesley, who set 'Methodist' revivalism in motion in England and the USA, fought vehemently against the 'sin' of slavery. Wesley published his book *Thoughts upon Slavery* in 1774. Beginning in 1784, slave owners were excommunicated by Methodists. In England many friends of Wesley who were involved in politics became active against slavery. The most famous of these is William Wilberforce (1759-1833).

William Wilberforce had been a representative in the British House of Commons since 1780. He converted to Evangelical Protestantism in 1784 on a trip through continental Europe and founded the *Abolition Society* in order to elevate morals and especially abolish the slave trade. In a Parliamentary meeting in 1789, Wilberforce, along with William Pitt, for the first time petitioned in the House of Commons to abolish the slave trade. Again in 1792 a petition was filed, this time successfully. Yet implementation was prevented due to war and the situation in the colonies. It was not until 1807 that an act of Parliament ended the British slave trade. Slave traders within the British sphere of control were viewed as pirates and punished. The United States of America followed, whereby beginning in 1808 the slave trade was forbidden.

At that point Wilberforce set his sights on implementing this prohibition in the rest of the civilized world. Upon his urging, Lord Castlereagh successfully raised this as an issue at the Congress of Vienna. Finally, there were agreements in which France, Spain, and Portugal obligated themselves to forbid the slave trade

---

[60]   See Unander, *Shattering*, pp. 24-26 and 36-40.

William Wilberforce, Bridgeman Art Gallery; Portrait: Wilberforce House, Hull Museum, Hull City Council; Painter: Karl Anton Hickel (1794)[61]

After the slave trade was abolished, Wilberforce finally became active in ostracizing and eliminating slavery itself. In 1816 he presented a motion in Parliament to reduce the number of slaves in the British West Indies. The government began preparing the emancipation of all slaves in 1823, and Wilberforce held impassioned speeches throughout the fierce debate until in 1825, due to health reasons, he had to retire. He died in 1833 and was buried in the church of the British crown, Westminster Abbey.

Slavery Today

Unfortunately, slavery still exists, even if in the meantime it is prohibited almost everywhere, lastly in Saudi Arabia in 1962 and in Oman in 1970. Slavery in Africa is flourishing around the Sahara, namely in Mauritania, Mali, Nigeria, Sudan, and Chad as it has in the past, whereby the owners are mostly Muslim Arabs and the slaves mostly 'blacks.' The number of slaves in Mauritania is estimated to be 100,000.

The oldest human rights organization in the world, the British organization *Anti-Slavery International*, reckons that there are 100 million slaves worldwide. In India and Pakistan, slaves primarily work in stone quarries, and in Pakistan alone the number of slaves is estimated at 20 million. In Thailand, Brazil, and India it is children who are above all enslaved, many of them in the prostitution industry. The most widely spread form of slavery today is a brutal form of debt servitude, by which families incur higher debts for their work implements than they receive in wages. Among the

---

[61] Http://upload.wikimedia.org/wikipedia/commons/e/eb/William_wilberforce.jpg (07.03.2011).

worst slavery is ironically found in the Dominican Republic amidst Haitians, although this is the only country in which African slaves were successful in acquiring control of the government. About one million slaves still work there on sugar plantations.

Excursus: The Death Penalty for Slave Traders in the Old Testament

The term translated 'slave' in the Old Testament is ambiguous, because it is all too easy to read into the Old Testament the cruel slavery conducted by the Greeks, Romans, Muslims, Europeans, and Americans. For this reason it is better to speak of 'debt servitude' or 'service,' and often of 'workers' instead of 'slave,' 'servant,' or 'footman.' The legal status of slaves/servants in Israel over against other peoples was remarkably good. They could ask for damages in the case of bodily harm, go to court, buy their freedom, etc.[62]

How did someone (lawfully) become a slave or servant in the Old Testament? It was in any event never lawful to become a slave through kidnapping or the sale of people, because the death penalty was required for such action: "Anyone who kidnaps another and either sells him or still has him when he is caught must be put to death" (Exodus 21:16). It should be emphasized that the New Testament writers did not overlook the mistakes of slavery. The Pauline list of law breakers includes slave traders (I Timothy 1:9-10, literally: 'people traders'). "John incorporates slavery into his analysis of wrongs which pervade Babylon: wrongs for which the city is judged (Rev 18:13)."[63] The same Paul who encouraged slaves to work hard and to maintain their Christian life could also write: ". . . although if you can gain your freedom, do so" (I Corinthians 7:21b). In Philemon Paul pleads for the release of a slave.

2. Genocide

Genocide under international Criminal Law

Genocide, first included within international criminal law, was increasingly made a punishable offense in many national legal systems. In 1948 the General Assembly of the United Nations produced a resolution in the

---

[62]   See details in Thomas Schirrmacher, *Ethik*, vol. 5, Hamburg: RVB, 2001[3], pp. 221-250.

[63]   Michael Parsons, "Slavery and the New Testament: Equality and Submissiveness", in: *Vox Evangelica* 18 (1988), p. 90.

"Convention on the Prevention and Punishment of the Crime of Genocide," which went into effect in 1951 and which was ratified by Germany in 1951, by Austria in 1955, and by Switzerland in 2000. The Convention defines genocide as "any of the following acts committed with intent to destroy, in whole or in part, a national, ethnical, racial or religious group, as such: (a) Killing members of the group; (b) Causing serious bodily or mental harm to members of the group; (c) Deliberately inflicting on the group conditions of life calculated to bring about its physical destruction in whole or in part; (d) Imposing measures intended to prevent births within the group; (e) Forcibly transferring children of the group to another group.

Within the framework of the United Nations and international law, genocide is the gravest offense. Moreover, and unlike a war of aggression, it is clearly defined and something for which international criminal courts and tribunals are used. It can also be prosecuted by countries other than those subject to it. Since the cases of genocide in Yugoslavia and Rwanda, for which international tribunals have been utilized, and since the formation of the International Court of Justice in Den Haag in 2003, the condemnation of genocide has increasingly taken on practical importance.

With this it is to be noted that it was not just the carrying out of genocide, but rather the intention to commit genocide which is sufficient for a charge. On the other hand, the sheer killing of many people belonging to a group, which is not done in a genocidal sense, is not yet considered to come under criminal law.

The Steps to Genocide

1. *Classification* – a particular group is distinguished from 'us.'

2. *Symbolization* – Hate symbols and terms of hatred stigmatize the group.

3. *Dehumanization* – A group is compared with sub-humans, apes, animals, viruses, etc.

4. *Polarizing Propaganda* – Propaganda provides the condition whereby genocide is seen as normal or unavoidable and can be supported.

5. *Organization* – The preconditions for genocide are created, e.g., via arming, the construction of camps, but also bureaucratically by compiling or registering the group.

6. *Extermination* – The actual murder occurs via mass killings or by depriving people of their basis for survival.

7. *Denial* – During and above all after extermination genocide is denied, ascribed to completely different perpetrators, or traced back to non-racist, alleged factors that can be otherwise explained

Examples of Genocide

Aborigines in Australia: The British settlement that began in 1788 led within 120 years to the almost complete extinction of the original inhabitants of Australia and neighboring islands. Although no official numbers are available, the estimates range from 250,000 to 750,000 Aborigines in 1788, which by 1911 had shrunk to 31,000. Genocide committed against Aborigines and their oppression ran through three phases. Up until about 1900 Aborigines were practically unprotected game and were driven off by the scores and hunted and killed as game. They were not considered people, but rather dangerous animals. As a result of massacres, the British government enacted a law in 1897 called the Aborigines Act, a law protecting the original inhabitants that had as a result geographical racial separation. Aborigines then began to live in enclosed remote woodlands and island areas, which they were not allowed to leave and into which no settlers could go. Beginning in the 1920s, an assimilation policy was also instated. The children of original inhabitants were taken from their parents (estimates for 1910-1970 range from 10% -30% of all children) and put in homes or with 'white' families, and later married to 'whites.' Whoever could demonstrate how 'white' he or she had become (via marriage or lifestyle) could apply for citizenship and the right to vote. It was not until 1996 that Aborigines received the right to vote, and it was not until the 1980s that racial segregation in the schools was repealed.

Genocide of Armenians in Turkey: "Prior to World War I, the largest indigenous[64] ethno-religious minorities were Armenians and Greeks, who accounted for 2.5 million and between 2.7 and 3 million people, respectively, in the Ottoman Empire. In the last decades of Ottoman-Turkish rule they, along with Aramaic speaking Christians (self designated: Syrio-Arameans, Assyrians, Chaldeans), became the sacrifices of state planned and directed massacres as well as deportations, which genocide research assesses as genocide according to the criteria of the UN Genocide Convention (1948). It was namely the genocide of 1.5 million Armenians of Ottoman citizenship, together with the massacre of Assyrians in Iraq in 1933, a prototypical genocide, which prompted the author of the UN Genocide Convention, Raphael Lemkin, as the legal adviser of the League of Nations, to introduce the draft of a corresponding international contractual framework into the League of Nations. He failed, however, due to the resistance of the delegation from Nazi Germany. While the Armenian population of the Ottoman Empire shrunk by three-fifths within two years (spring 1915 to February 1917), the extermination of the Greek Orthodox

---

[64] I.e., those originally living in a region.

population lasted a decade and was executed at varying locations. It is for that reason called a cumulative genocide."[65]

National Socialism 1933-1945: The "Holocaust" (from the Greek term for 'completely incinerated,' i.e., 'burnt offering') or shoah (Hebrew for 'disaster,' 'great catastrophe') is what one calls the genocide of at least 5.6 million to 6.3 million Jews during the time of National Socialism. World War II cost the lives of 15.8 million non-Germans and 4.2 million German soldiers and members of paramilitary units, as well as 15.8 million non-German civilian victims and 500,000 German civilian victims of aerial warfare. 2.27 million members of the German civil population died as they were forcibly displaced from the East. And all of these are rather low estimates. Especially alarming is that out of this total the direct number of National Socialistic crimes not included as actions of war according to the current state of research is 13 million people, among them 6 million Jews, 3.3 million Soviet prisoners of war, 2.5 Christian Poles, a further 784,000 non-German victims from all over Europe in concentration camps and work camps, 296,000 Sinti und Roma (gypsies), 100,000 mentally ill and handicapped as victims of euthanasia and 130,000 non-Jewish Germans involved in political or religious resistance. I have listed all of these numbers, because it is also meant to remove any basis sought for the so-called 'Auschwitz lie.' The 'Auschwitz lie' is a contentious term by which those who deny the reality of the Holocaust maintain that it is impossible to think that around 6 million Jews were killed.

Mass Extermination by the Khmer Rouge: During the reign of terror of the Khmer Rouge in Cambodia from 1975-1979, it is estimated that out of a total population of 7 million, 1.4 million to 2.2 million inhabitants were killed. One-half were killed in death camps and the other half through forced labor in the rice fields or through starvation. The mass killings are termed 'auto-genocide' by experts, since the Cambodian people almost killed themselves off. Many researchers view the mass murders of the Khmer Rouge not as genocide but as something purely politically motivated. Indeed, in such case there was still among the mass murders genocide with respect to a portion of the killings, so it can be said that almost all Vietnamese in the country were killed out of a racist motivation.

Genocide in Rwanda: Between April and July 1994 the army, police, and civilian population of the Hutu majority killed approximately 800,000 to 1 million people. In so doing, they killed 75% of the Tutsi minority living in Rwanda as well as moderate Hutus, who did not participate in the

---

[65] Tessa *Hofmann*, „Wer in der Türkei Christ ist ... zahlt einen Preis dafür", in: *Märtyrer 2007*, Bonn: VKW, pp. 161-162.

genocide. Neighbors killed their neighbors with machetes, and the remaining Tutsis fled to the Congo, Burundi, and Uganda. The UN's own criminal court has met since 1996, and hundreds of thousands of victims have been dug up and buried. Typical for the senselessness of racism is the fact that the Hutu and Tutsi are not really different people groups. Rather, they are social stratifications. At least it can be said that no difference at all was made between Hutu and Tutsi prior to 1916. Germans and then the Belgian colonial masters relied on the richer Tutsis in order to control the country, and they additionally considered them to be Aryan. When independence was granted in 1962, the Belgians saw to it that the Hutu, who represented the majority of the population, received power. In 1994 the accidental death of the Hutu president provided extremists the pretense for seizing power and conducting genocide. The international community looked on silently for three months, until the military arm of the Tutsi resistance conquered the capital of Kigali with the support of neighboring countries.[66]

Srebrenica Massacre: In July 1995 up to 8,000 Bosnians, primarily men and boys between the ages of 12 and 77, were killed in the area of Srebrenica by members of the Serbian army, police, and paramilitary. In 2007 these actions were determined by the International Court of Justice to be genocide.

Genocide in Darfur: Since 2003 there have been armed conflicts between black African tribes in Darfur in the Sudan and the Arab-Muslim central regime in Khartoum. The rebel movement calls for co-determination and the development of their region. Against this movement the central government has taken steps with, above all, the local militia consisting of mounted Arab Nomads (Janjaweed). Up to the present 400,000 people have died and 2.5 million have fled within Sudan or into neighboring countries. The destruction of villages, massacres, and rape are the order of the day. 'Black African' and 'Arab' are actually senseless categories, since only 2% of all inhabitants of the Sudan are of Arab descent. The conflict goes back to earlier rivalries in the slave trade and to economic contrasts, whereby the Fur and Masalite were settled farmers and the 'Arab' Baggara and Zaghawa were nomadic stockbreeders.

Unwanted Genocide due to Racism

Not every actual case of genocide is desired, at least not when looking at history. Often what was sought was only the dependence or compliance of an ethnic group, and yet people died due to poor living conditions or unforeseen factors.

---

[66] A good evaluation is found in Delacampagne, *Geschichte*, pp. 265-270.

An example is the widespread death that occurred among Indians in Middle and South America and in North America at the beginning of the European discovery and conquest of America. Even if there are several examples of the slaughter of small groups of Indians, the shrinking of the Indian population by 90% is not something that can be traced back to specific murders or cases of being killed off. Rather, it above all, has to do with epidemics that were brought in and against which the Indians were not immune, the danger and spreading of which was not known until centuries later. In addition to this, the Indian physical constitution was such that the slave work in the fields or in mines, which the Europeans and the Africans survived, was not something with which the Indians were able to cope.[67]

In any event, the number of Europeans in Middle and South America was too small for there to be genocide. Additionally, the Europeans' goal was to rule over people and become rich, not to eradicate people – all without wishing to sugarcoat their racism.

In North America it was not until much later, after the number of Indians had been decimated and 'black' slaves had been seen to be much more able to survive and more easy to exploit, that the Indians were 'in the way' of the European settlers. The attempts at a solution were no longer through genocide but rather through forced displacement to reservations. However, that was able to again lead to race based murders in cases where those who would not acquiesce were submitted to bad living conditions or were warred against.

Threatened Peoples

"The number of peoples or ethnicities cannot even be approximated. The same thing applies here that applies to the number of languages. It is a question of definition, whether one, for example, counts Arabs as a people or does so with each Arabic tribe or each Arabic nation (Syrians, Lebanese, Jordanians, etc.). The number of ethnicities is greatest in Asia and Africa (in each from 1,800 to 2,000 in number). In Europe, according to the way the counting is conducted, one arrives at a number of 120 to 150 (without immigrants)."[68] In light of the approximate 200 nations worldwide it is clear that most of the ethnicities of this world do not have their own country. Many peoples live in peace with others in multiethnic states, but a large number live as threatened ethnic minorities ruled by majority peo-

---

[67] See Delacampagne, *Geschichte*, pp. 106-111, who suggests speaking of 'ethno-cide' instead of 'genocide' in this case.

[68] Stegner, *Taschenatlas*, p. 13.

ples, experiencing everything from light discrimination all the way up to attempts to assimilate them completely or to force their displacement or extermination.

I regret it deeply that due to the limited scope of this book, no picture can be given of some of these threatened peoples beyond examples provided at other junctures, and not in the form found in the encyclopedias mentioned in the bibliography.

Excursus: Diversity of Cultures in the Bible

God is the creator of all people, because "from one man he made every nation of men, that they should inhabit the whole earth . . . (Acts 17:26a; comp. Deuteronomy 32:7-9; Psalm 74:17; 86:9). For that reason a Christian loves people of all cultures and respects the differentness of other cultures (Revelation 1:6-8; Psalm 66:8).

Many Christians see the differences between cultures in a negative light and understand them as a result of sin. For them it is a consequence of the judgment of God due to the confusion of languages at the building of the Tower of Babel (Genesis 11:1-9). With the confusion of languages God wanted to achieve that which he had before given to mankind as a command, namely the proliferation of mankind over the whole earth ("fill the earth," Genesis 1:28; 9:1) and with it the splitting of humanity not only into a diversity of families and peoples but also into vocations, abilities, and cultures. With the construction of the Tower of Babel a unified world culture was to have been created. This has always been the goal of Satan, as is shown in the book of Revelation and in the person of the Antichrist in the Old and New Testaments. And this is what is said of the 'beast,' which has his power from the 'dragon' (Revelation 13:1-10): "He was given power to make war . . . And he was given authority over every tribe, people . . ."

God and his word guarantee the unity of the world but not, however, a visible structure on earth. God 'scattered' people "over the face of the whole earth" (Genesis 11:9b). Extending from the Sons of Noah, "came the people who were scattered over the earth" (Genesis 9:19) and so the "nations" were "spread out" (Genesis 10:5). In this way the individual peoples can be explained through lines of descent (Genesis 10: 1-32), at the end of which it can be said: "From these nations spread out over the earth after the flood (Genesis 10:32b).

It is no accident that the drifting apart of cultures begins when families drift apart. Every family has its own culture, and God has so created man that without exception one's own children even create their own little culture, which always differs at least some from that of the parents. It is a process that over generations has far-reaching consequences. These different cultures that children have are enhanced when children marry children from other families and, with them, marry into different cultures. God consciously mixes different cultures and influences in marriage. Social and cultural conflicts are not automatically an expression of moral failures. Rather, they are normal and are a consequence of a diversity desired by God.

Already in the Old Testament, God made it repeatedly known that he was thinking about the salvation of all peoples (Genesis 12:3; Isaiah 49:6, etc.). Jonah's mission exemplifies the universal nature of divine salvation as early as Old Testament times. Pentecost makes it clear that the church of Jesus extends beyond all cultural and language barriers. For this reason the church was laid out multi-culturally (Revelation 5:9-10; 7:9; 10:11; 11:9; 13:7; 14:6; 17:15; Daniel 7:13-14; Ephesians 2:11-19).

3. Racial Segregation

Racial segregation means the forced and firmly set separation of people groups defined as 'races' in all areas of life. Typical segregation would include prohibition on marriages between members of different 'races,' physically separate residential areas as well as separate public facilities such as schools, universities, public transportation, restaurants, beaches, and toilets, whereby the facilities for the leading group are as a rule better equipped.

The most prominent examples are Germany's Third Reich from 1933 to 1945, the USA from 1890 until the middle of the 1960s, and South Africa beginning in 1900 and above all from 1948 until 1990. In the USA one speaks about racial segregation as the time beginning after the end of slavery. Rhodesia (at first 'white' against 'black,' and now 'black' against 'white') and Australia (against the Aborigines until 1966) are additional examples. In a certain sense Northern Ireland also belonged within this group up until a short time ago.

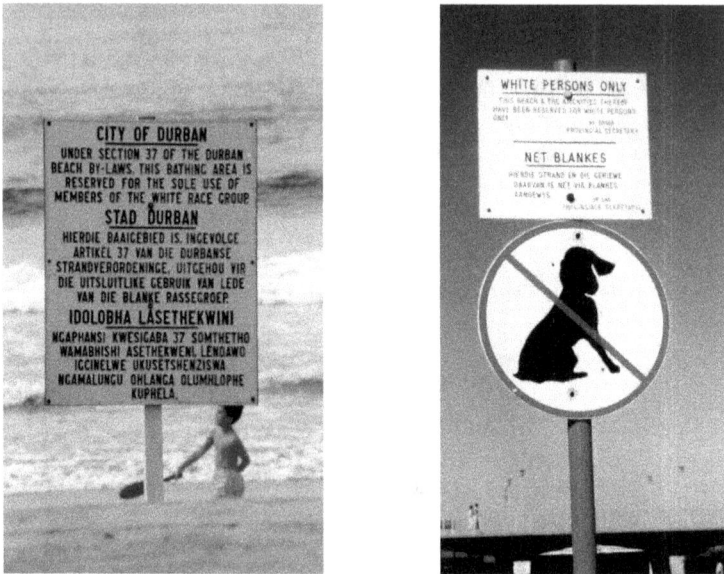

Illustration 5: Apartheid on the beach of Durban, South Africa, 1989[69]

USA

The history of America has three central racist themes. These are the expulsion of the Indians, the deportation of African slaves, and as a counterpart thereto, the establishment of the dominance of 'whites.' In addition to this are further areas of racism that can be named but never took on the same proportions, for instance, the prohibition against the immigration of gypsies, suspicion towards Irish Catholics and later towards Spanish-speaking immigrants, restricting immigration from Southeastern Europe, and widespread anti-Semitism until the middle of the 20th century. It is naturally impossible to present a history of the USA at this point.

In the South of the USA an officially racist justification for slavery first developed in the 1830s, when the anti-slavery movement began in the northern section of the USA. With the victory of the northern states in the American Civil War, and along with it the end of slavery in the southern states, traditional racial segregation, above all in the southern states, was placed into question. Subsequently, a number of southern states, as well as states bordering them, passed laws that legally anchored racial segregation.

---

[69]   Http://de.wikipedia.org/w/index.php?title=Datei:DurbanSign1989.jpg&filetime
       stamp=20080315054520 (07.03.2011)
       Http://de.wikipedia.org/w/index.php?title=Datei:Apartheid.jpg&filetimestamp=20
       070731153433 (07.03.2011)

The Supreme Court in the USA *de facto* confirmed the laws in 1896, in that it held racial segregation as permissible, insofar as the facilities and services that were made available were equivalent (*separate but equal*).

In 1948, shortly after World War II, the abolishment of racial discrimination began in the US Army and in federal service, and additional legal improvement followed. In 1954 there was a Supreme Court decision against racial segregation in education. But it was in the wake of the American Civil Rights Movement in the 1960s, representatively connected with the name of the Baptist Pastor Martin Luther King, that racial segregation laws were abolished little by little. In 1964 the Civil Rights Act of that same year rescinded all remaining laws against 'blacks.' It was not until 1967 that the Supreme Court lifted the prohibition on marriages between blacks and whites. The legal equality of the 11% of the population of the USA that is 'black' was complete, but the consequences of earlier racism have by no means been removed.

At this point it should be noted that Europeans often display an almost racist view of the USA, as if they themselves are free from racism and the USA is incurably racist. Richard Heringer writes in this connection: "That Barack Obama, as a black American, for the first time has a realistic chance to become President of the United States of America is in fact a great incision in history, and he is thus highly recognized. In our reporting, however, almost all attention is given to the question of the degree to which Obama's being black is in the final analysis an insurmountable handicap for American voters. Strangely enough that appears to be ambiguous . . . In order to measure what has been achieved in the United States in the past three or four decades in this respect . . . counter questions suffice: Could you imagine that in the 2009 *Bundestag* elections a German of Turkish ancestry could be nominated as the leading candidate of one of the largest political parties? That a politician with a Moroccan father and an Arab name could challenge Nicolas Sarkozy for the office of President of France? Or that a politician of African ancestry would be considered for the post of the President of the European Commission? . . . With respect to diversity as well as to immense efforts to overcome racism in the public sphere or at least to socially discourage it, the USA is far beyond Europeans – not to speak of other parts of the world."[70]

---

[70]   Richard Herzinger, „Obamas Problem ist nicht der Rassismus", in: *Die Welt*, June 11, 2008.

South Africa

"The one racist regime that survived the Second World War and the Cold War was the South African, which did not in fact come to fruition until the advent of apartheid in 1948,"[71] even if apartheid had a political history in the special segregation of 'blacks' into so-called 'homelands.' If in 1948 the descendants of the British had the say in South Africa, in 1948 it was the racist Boors of Dutch descent who won the elections and introduced strict racial segregation. It in turn was divided into two types of segregation, Petty Apartheid and Grand Apartheid.

Petty Apartheid meant racial segregation in the public service area, such as, for instance the prohibition against blacks' entering public parks, separate compartments in public transportation or separate schools. City halls, hospitals, postal buildings, banks, and toilets mostly had two entrances, one for 'whites' and one for other 'races.' Additionally, one knew by word of mouth in which restaurants, etc. 'blacks' would not be served. Naturally, along with this came exclusive voting rights for 'whites.'

Grand apartheid meant the so-called homeland policy, which involved the settlement of most 'blacks' in alleged small states within South Africa. In addition to this, there were separate residential areas in each city and village corresponding to skin color ('white,' 'black,' 'colored/Asian').

Apartheid included a huge administrative apparatus. It is estimated that 4 million 'blacks' were arrested due to missing residence permits. Millions of people were resettled as a result of the 1952 *Native Resettlement Act*, which was a challenge administratively as well as for the police. Protests against the act necessitated mass arrests and required large prisons or camps. The destruction of large existing settlements, because they were held to be illegal or were used to make room for white neighborhoods, required an enormous infrastructure.

In my opinion, the story of apartheid in South Africa is still not over, not only because the earlier Apartheid under the 'whites' still continues to have effects and decades of neglect of large parts of the population are not quickly made up for. Rather, many 'colored' and people of Indian descent continue to be discriminated against and a severe 'black' racism not only against 'whites' but against alleged immigrants from other African countries has spread. Old antagonism between Xhosa and Zulu, etc. have broken out again. "Whoever looks at South Africa today will conclude that things are not good in the country. Corruption and nepotism, lies and black racism rage in a country which after the end of apartheid stood for the hope

---

[71]   Fredrickson, *Rassismus*, p. 11.

of another Africa, for a continent in which blacks and whites could live in a democratic relationship next to each other and where a still oppressed majority is in the position to guide the fortunes of the country into a framework in accordance with a rule of law. Still, nothing of the like indicates that these expectations are being fulfilled."[72] There hardly would have been the support of appalling dictators in Zimbabwe or in the Sudan under Nelson Mandela. "Still, almost ten years after he left office as South Africa's President, there are more and more signs indicating that the, in the meantime ninety-year-old, was an anomaly."[73]

Zimbabwe (prior South Rhodesia) became independent under the white racist leader Ian Smith in 1965. It lived for 15 years with strict racial segregation until the United Nations forced multiracial elections in 1980. As a result Robert Gabriel Mugabe (b. 1924) came out as a winner, and he immediately transformed the country into a malicious dictatorship. In what was initially an understandable effort to bring about a new distribution of land for the benefit of 'blacks,' the end result was that a large portion of 'whites,' as well as members of all competing tribes, were driven out or killed.

4. The Combination of Racism with other Factors

The Combination of Racism with Religion, Politics, and Language

Racism is often inseparably combined with other types of condemnation and oppression of unwanted groups of people. It is often racism that provides the ideological justification for completely different conflicts, and it is often so that conflicts finally lead to a racist hardening of an existing conflict.

A typical example is the form of anti-Zionism against **Israel** that is a variation of anti-Semitism directed against Jews. This form of anti-Zionism wants to see Israel left without a Jewish state in Palestine, even if a solution for the Palestinians is going to be found. (There are other definitions of anti-Zionism, e.g. rejecting zionistic claims, that all Palestine belongs to Israel according to God's command.) But what is the subject of the hatred in this case? Does it have to do with Jews as a race? Does it have to do with Judaism as a religion in contrast to Islam? Or with the liberal political system of Israel? Is it envy about Israel's economic successes? Does it have to do with the Jews as a race? It stands to reason, because otherwise

---

[72]   Jacques Schuster, „Der Fall Südafrikas: Einst Mandelas Wunderland, heute Sittenverfall", in: *Die* Welt, August 6, 2008.

[73]   *Idem.*

the Arabic edition of *Mein Kampf* would not be a bestseller, which by the way renders 'anti-Semitism' with 'anti-Judaism,' because the Nazis naturally did not mean the Arabs, who are likewise 'Semites.' The same combination is naturally found in its opposite form in the attitude of many Israelis toward **Palestinians**.

Or let's take **Turkey** since Kemal Ataturk. Turkey is built upon a strong sense of Turkish nationalism. But is it *religiously* based? Whoever is not a Muslim is not a true Turk, and even non-Sunnite Turkish Muslims such as the Alevites are persecuted. Is it based on *language*? Kurdish, Armenian and Assyrian should be extinguished as native languages. Is it racially justified? Kurds, Armenians and Assyrians are seen as contaminants. It is really all of this together, a nationalism, that should hold the people of the country together. That Ataturk was himself of Albanian descent exemplarily demonstrates – as we have said before –that most often such nationalism has little to do with reality.

The Combination of Racism and Religion (Iraq, Vietnam, Ireland)

There are many examples of the combination of racism and religious persecution. In **Iraq** the long established Christian population is under persecution. The Assyrio-Chaldean and other Christian ethnicities, such as the Armenians, are also opposed. This is because they are a non-Arab minority as well as due to the fact that they are Christians and not Muslims. Out of what used to be 650,000 Christians who had lived in Iraq for almost 200 years, three quarters of them had been driven out of the country.[74]

In **Vietnam** the government is persecuting Montagnards – French for 'mountain dwellers' – in the central Vietnamese highlands, because these people have turned to Christianity in large numbers. These people were pushed into the mountains at the beginning of the 20th century. They are completely cut off from economic development and remain impoverished. Persecuted under the communists, about 2 million Montagnards turned to Christianity. Their fertile land was largely unlawfully allocated to the Kinh Vietnamese. Their faith has aroused the suspicion that they are working for foreign powers. A portion of the Montagnards fled to Cambodia because of expropriation, imprisonment, torture, and the prohibition against practicing their religion.

From 1969 to 1998 Protestant British and Catholic Irish fought violently in **Northern Ireland**, respectively using small armed militia on both sides. The industrialized northeastern areas of Northern Ireland and almost all

---

[74] Gesellschaft für bedrohte Völker, „Die größte Christenverfolgung der Gegenwart", in: *Märtyrer 2007*, VKW: Bonn, 2007, pp. 161-162.

larger cities became Protestant, while the rural western areas were dominated by Catholics. The Northeast is more highly industrialized than the rural West. Both groups emerged from long standing Irish, on the one hand, and from Scottish and English settlers who colonized Ireland, on the other hand. The conflict is what determined the course of daily life, caused the separation of residential areas in the cities, and cost almost 4,000 civilians their lives.

The Combination of Racism and Language (Belgium)

An example of the combination of racism with linguistic and economic questions is **Belgium**. The Dutch speaking Flemish (60%), primarily in the north, the Walloons and other French speaking inhabitants, above all in the south and in Brussels (40%), the German-speaking minority in the east, as well as the capital Brussels in the center with two official languages, are actually only held together by the crown. In spite of advancing decentralization since the 1970s, and the transformation of the country into a federal state in 1993, conflicts and national crises have not come to a halt.[75] Since the collapse of the mining industry, the French-speaking part is significantly poorer. This is a reason there is a strong separatist movement among the Flemish, one that would avoid 'feeding' the Walloons any longer.

It is interesting and at the same time typical that the alleged ethnic conflict is considered to have begun at the earliest with the founding of the Kingdom of Belgium in 1830, when actually it occurred at the end of the 19th century when the Flemish in French-speaking Belgium rediscovered their Dutch language. Up to that time, French had been the language of education for all people.

Justification of Racism with Religion (India)

In his *History of Racism*, Imanuel Geiss views the Indian caste system as "the oldest form of quasi-racist structures,"[76] which began at the latest with the conquest of Northern India by the Aryans around 1500 B.C. "Light skinned conquerors forced dark-skinned subjects as 'slaves' into apartheid in a race-caste society, which could not be held in its original form, but led to an extreme fragmentation and sealing off of life into separated castes for many matters related to vocation, place of residential, eating, and mar-

---

[75] Comp. de.wikipedia.org/wiki/Flämisch-wallonischer_Konflikt und Frank Berge/ Alexander Grasse, *Belgien – Zerfall oder föderales Zukunftsmodell? – Der flämisch-wallonische Konflikt und die Deutschsprachige Gemeinschaft*, Opladen: Leske + Budrich, 2003.

[76] Imanuel Geiss, *Geschichte des Rassismus*, Frankfurt: Suhrkamp, 1993, p.49.

riage."[77] The conference on anti-racism held by the United Nations in Durban (South Africa) in March 2001 vocally condemned racism on the basis of the caste system as apartheid, but it did not lead to any formal resolution against India.

It is astonishing that this type of religiously based racism has continued in India for 3,500 years. We will limit ourselves to the lowest class in the caste system and not take into account that in India, in opposition to the constitution, many 'scheduled tribes' are neglected and spurned.

'Dalit' is the self-designation of the descendents of original Indian inhabitants, who for racist reasons were excluded as 'untouchables' ('pariahs') from the caste system of the militant indo-European conquerors. In our country they were often incorrectly referred to in earlier times as 'casteless.' The number of Hindu Dalits is estimated at 240 million, of which 160 million are Hindus, and the rest Buddhists and Christians, that is, almost one quarter of the Indian population. Up to the present they are discriminated against by Indians belonging to various castes, scorned, exploited, held as slaves, beaten, deprived of their possessions and their land, and forced to conduct the lowest forms of work. Women are often in part even publicly raped without any consequences. Presently, 800,000 Dalits in India have to empty latrines with their bare hands.

Admittedly the 1949 constitution of the Republic of India forbids discrimination on the basis of caste and ethnicity. However, in practice, all such measures have had little success. In 1956 B. R. Ambedkar (1891-1956) initiated a mass conversion of Dalits to Buddhism, and additional mass conversions to Buddhism and Christianity followed. However, this only worsened the situation of the Dalits, especially since Dalits stop receiving social welfare as soon as they have officially become Christians.

---

[77]   Geiss, p. 49

III. The Situation in Germany

1. Gypsies

Since the 15th century, the German term *Zigeuner* ("gypsy") or a similar term in all other European languages (e.g., French *tsigane*, Italian *zingaro*, Turkish *cingene*) has designated a widely fragmented group of approximately 15 million people. This group consists of immigrant peoples, Roma and Sinti, who came from India over the Balkans to Europe in the 14th and 15 centuries. In addition to them, there were smaller European groups such as the *Jenisch*, who lived with the Roma and Sinti or had a similar lifestyle.

It is presumed that in the 9th to 11th centuries these peoples were displaced by Arab conquerors from Punjab in India and used as soldiers and slaves in the Eastern Roman Empire. After that they moved out of Turkey into the Balkans. The history of the Zigeuner ("gypsies") is a thousand-year story of racist disdain and oppression on almost all continents.

The first persecution of the gypsies is known to have come from the Romanian Wallachia and Moldavian principalities, where from the 14th until the 19th centuries Roma were enslaved, imprisoned, displaced, and segregated. The disdain for gypsies is still strongest there, and it is recognizable in the pogroms that occurred at the beginning of the 1990s shortly after the fall of the Berlin Wall.

Until approximately 1500, gypsies lived largely unmolested in the rest of Europe, especially since migrations were also widespread among other people groups. In 1498 the imperial princes and bishops at the Imperial Diet at Freiburg declared that all *Zigeuner* were spies for the Turks and enemies of Christianity. For that reason they were condemned. This was a one-off event in German legal history prior to National Socialism that fed on the hysterical fear of Turks. It is also a classic example of how racism develops.

In the 18th and 19th centuries *Zigeuner* was a defining term by the police, which was used in laws and ordinances against 'vagrant peoples.' Since more than 90% of Roma were settled down in Europe (not wandering), they were not much in evidence. It was the small portion of such people, who crossed borders in wandering groups, that came into people's field of vision. Since 1871 German law has spoken of the 'gypsy menace.'

In the 19th century the idea had spread so much that Roma were a group that belonged together racially and lived from theft and deception that immigration into the United States of America and Latin American countries was forbidden in 1880 and 1885. By the way, even in Malta and Denmark, where there are no 'gypsies,' a good portion of the population oppose 'gypsies,' as a recent European Union study has shown.

For decades there has been a refusal to speak about the genocide of 300,000 Roma and Sinti during the Third Reich, even after the fact of the genocide of Jews had long been accepted. The German Federal Supreme Court still ruled in 1956 that the persecution of gypsies under National Socialism was not racist in nature, but rather was aimed at the "asocial characteristics of the gypsies."[78]

Roma range from light skinned to dark skinned – sometimes within the same family – and at the same time they can consist of Orthodox, Catholics, Protestants, Muslims, Jews, and atheists. For outsiders, some of them are easily identified because of their skin color and are stopped at borders. Most of them, however, are not able to be differentiated from other Europeans.

In Germany the Central Council of Sinti and Roma disapproves of the designation 'gypsy' because of its ideological liability and its use in the Third Reich, while the less representative Sinti Alliance of Germany comes out for a 'value neutral' continued use of the term.

2. Anti-Semitism

The first anti-Semitism was found among the Greeks and Egyptians beginning in the 3rd century B.C. The "Invention of Judaism as a race in 1492"[79] took place in Spain, where Jews who converted to Christianity were nevertheless harshly persecuted due to alleged deception and conspiratorial intentions. Judaism was now no longer a religion but rather an indication of ancestry. After a long development, Eugen Dühring (1833-1921) drew the conclusion: Jewish baptism is not the solution, because it is not a question of religion, but rather of 'race' or 'race harmfulness,' respectively. It is hardly surprising that churches did not even stand up for and defend baptized Jews.

The Swiss government writes in this connection: "The term anti-Semitism, which was coined by Wilhelm Marr in 1879, designates enmity against Jews, who are construed and perceived as a homogenous 'race.' The development of such a racial term occurred in the course of the 19th century against the backdrop of an increasingly scientific approach as well as a decline in religious interpretations. Racist anti-Semitism is superim-

---

78 Quoted by Hund, *Rassismus: Konstruktion*, p. 75.
79 Geulen, *Geschichte*, p. 38.

posed upon historical anti-Judaism, which goes back a long way and stands for the religiously characterized enmity toward Jews . . . what is viewed as unalterable and fixed features of differentiation and stereotypes relating to the 'Jewish race' were used from then on as an instrument of segregation and discrimination. The anti-Semitism that came up in the 19th century in bourgeois circles as well as in the working class was in the first place a reaction to the entry of Jewish citizens into the social and political life of (Western) Europe . . . Features of anti-Semitism are the notion of a 'Jewish world conspiracy' and the fact that 'the Jews' have to be held out as the scapegoats for social, political, and societal evils."[80]

Nowadays European anti-Semitism primarily consists of some forms of anti-Zionism directed against the state of Israel (but see p. 65!) or in the continuation of the idea of Jewish conspiracy theories that have to be held out repeatedly to explain the appearance of anti-Semitism. It is thus parroted that Christians were forbidden to conduct money lending and for that reason the Jews took this line of business and became unpopular as a result of their involvement in it. Still, the picture of the Jewish 'usurer' arose at the end of the 14th century and the beginning of the 15th century after the grand epoch of international Jewish money dealing had long ended. In England the Jews had been displaced or driven underground as early as 1290 by the King. The advent of anti-Semitism did not cause any interruption in this. And in the 600 years since 1400 surely no one has analyzed whether actually it was only Jews who were allowed to lend money or whether other alleged historical truths about Jews are actually backed by any evidence.

3. National Socialism

The Uniqueness of Racism in the Third Reich

In the morning hours of June 6, 1941 Hitler attacked the Soviet Union "with the biggest fire storm of all time and with the strongest offensive armed force in military history."[81] Under the disguise of a horrible war for Lebensraum (living space) in the East, millions of Jews, gypsies and other 'non-Aryans' were killed. Hitler and his myrmidons put their racist worldview into practice in the shadows of war as an extermination, a 'Holocaust.' The 'Aryan' racism, along with anti-Semitism and anti-Gypsyism

---

[80] Eidgenössische Kommission gegen Rassismus, http://www.ekr-cfr.ch/themen/ 00023/00025/index.html?lang=de.

[81] Ralph Giordano, *Wenn Hitler den Krieg gewonnen hätte: Die Pläne der Nazis nach dem Endsieg*, Hamburg: Rasch und Röhring, 1989[2], p. 44.

has its roots in almost all European cultures, but it finds its bloody consummation in 'Germanic' racism. "Hitler only had two true goals, one relating to foreign policy and one relating to racial policy. Under his rule, Germany had to conquer new areas for living space in the East, and he had to remove the Jews. The state and its constitution, domestic, economic, and social policy, the party, their program and their ideology – everything was a means to this dual end."[82]

National Socialism was in its racism and genocide uniquely abominable. "I maintain ... that the national socialistic murder of Jews was unique because never before had a nation decided and announced via the authority of its leader in power that a particular group of people including the elderly, women, children, and infants was to be killed off as completely as possible and that this resolution was to be put into action with all possible state instruments of power."[83]

Something else differentiates National Socialism from most racist systems. While for instance the Indian caste system, the enslavement of black Africans by Arab lords, the apartheid in South Africa, or racial segregation in the southern part of the Unites States provided respective ideological justifications for a longstanding power structure, National Socialism built upon centuries-old prejudices and not on an actually present separation of society into Jews and non-Jews, apart from the Sinti and Roma. Jews were fully integrated into society and racial differentiation was not self-evident.

Hitler's Race Religion

"The core of the National Socialist worldview ... has been oft described. According to this worldview, history is a story of racial wars. The blond race is called to rule over the earth as the 'highest image of the Lord;' and yet the race sees itself under growing pressure from the inferior mixed breed races, in particular the Jews, which threatened the world with subjugation and destruction as the largest opposing force ... On the one hand, it is not only a historical mandate to fight and bring liquidation, but, on the other hand, it was a mandate to maintain the costly basin of Nordic blood via breeding and racial hygiene that would have the consecration and

---

[82]   *Op. cit.*, p.93.

[83]   Eberhard Jäckel, „Die elende Praxis der Untersteller", in: *Historikerstreit. Die Dokumentation der Kontroverse um die Einmaligkeit der nationalsozialistischen Judenvernichtung*, München: Piper, 1987, p. 118.

legitimization of a divine command since it would fulfill the plan of creation . . ."[84]

That Hitler directly combines God with a social Darwinistic fight for survival upon a racial ideological base,[85] which is seen most clearly when he refers to the 'Creator' (and similar expressions) . . . The German people received from the Creator the 'mandate' to reshape the world, for a "historical revision of unique proportions was given to us by the Creator."

When Hitler mentioned that "God [has] given me my blood," he did not mean, or at least he did not mean primarily, his creation as an individual being, but rather the creation of Aryan or German 'blood,' i.e., the blood of the race or of the people. That which God has created can for that reason only be a "commandment from God." Also, on account of this, racial egoism may "not be seen as not well-pleasing to God," since if God had not desired the involvement of the German race, "God [would not have] created me as a German." Whoever "destroys [God's] work" destroys the "creation of the Lord" and with that "declares war . . . on God's will."

The mixing of the races is, hence, the quintessential 'sin' against creation. However, Christianity is also rebellion and "protest against the creation," insofar as it rejects the necessity of killing in the fight for survival and, for instance, also rejects euthanasia. Christianity's lack of focus on race puts it into a position of opposition against the Creator, for instance when missionary work leads to accepting 'inferior' people. For Hitler it is a sin against the will of the eternal Creator, . . . if hundreds of thousands . . . of his most well gifted beings decay in the present day proletarian quagmire, while Hottentots and Zulu kaffirs are trained up for . . . church vocations."

It can be assumed that the connection between thinking about theistic creation and biological evolution, in the sense that God created the fight for survival, was not a feature distinctive to Hitler. Rather, it was something that was in circulation at his time in various forms. The odd mixture that came into play with Hitler, one of enlightenment and the priority of science, along with belief in God and the God-willed fostering of the evolution of the races, was at that time to some extent in the air, even if it cannot alone explain why this combination had such brutal consequences for Hitler and not for other theistically enlightened social Darwinists.

---

[84] Joachim Fest et. al., *Hitler*, München: Heyne, 1980, p. 15.

[85] All documentation for the following section is found in Schirrmacher, *Hitlers Kriegsreligion*, vol. 1, pp. 246-258 and vol. 2, pp. 352-381.

4. Right-wing Extremism in German-speaking Countries today

Right-wing Extremism in Germany

The University of Leipzig has repeatedly conducted surveys for the Friedrich Ebert Foundation, which is closely allied with the German SPD political party, regarding the spread of right-wing extremist attitudes.[86] The numbers are reproduced below, although they are not significantly meaningful.

Right-Wing Extremist Attitudes in western and eastern sections of Germany, Fall 2006

	Total	West	East
In favor of Dictatorship	4.8	4.4	6.5
Chauvinistic	19.3	20.1	16.1
Hostile to Foreigners	26.7	25.7	30.6
Anti-Semitic	8.4	9.5	4.2
Socially Darwinistic	4.5	4.0	6.2
Find National Socialism trivial	4.1	4.6	2.0

What is there to criticize about such numbers and almost all similar investigations? There are three questions that relate to each of the five topics, but a positive answer to each question could just as easily be given by a left-wing extremist. Absurd charges against Jews are not only found in the rightist camp. It is not only right-wing extremists who want a dictatorship and a strong man. Social Darwinism is also a component of the Marxist worldview. The German politician Oskar Lafontaine has gone hunting for votes with references of hostility to foreigners and alleged domination by foreign influences. Additionally, some of the questions are asked in a manner that, taken by themselves, naïve citizens would agree with, for instance when a question is asked as to whether Germany receives too little attention in international politics.

---

[86] Oliver Decker et. al., *Ein Blick in die Mitte: Zur Entstehung rechtsextremer und demokratischer Einstellungen* in *Deutschland*, Berlin: Friedrich-Ebert-Stiftung, 2008.

It has been shown from the many surveys that only have to do with right-wing or left-wing extremism that they are always one-sided. When both are polled and analyzed together, the analyses are senseless.

It is to be briefly noted at this point that the fight against racism is made more difficult when one only assumes it is a matter suspected of a political opponent. Without wanting to constrict the fight against right-wing radical racism in one way or another, racism can be bound together with each and every political ideology, with leftist political positions and left-wing extremism. Oskar Lafontaine's racist statements regarding Poland and Southeast Europe demonstrate this in a relatively harmless example, while the Soviet Union's imperialism and the Marxism of the 'white' hater Robert Mugabe exhibit are its violent outgrowth.

While there are hardly any reliable numbers available as to how many Germans have racist or right-wing extremist attitudes, and most truly high numbers only come from the political left, the numbers of active racists and right-wing extremists look more reliable. This is due to the fact that in Germany, surveillance of right-wing extremism is the task of the offices of constitutional protection of the states and of the federal government, which is independent of whether it is the CDU/CSU parties or the SPD party that heads government. In these cases, similar results have been found over longer periods of time.

According to the 2007 report on constitutional protection published by the German Interior Ministry, there are presently 4,400 neo-Nazis as well as 14,200 members in the right-wing extremist NPD (National Democratic Party of Germany) and DVU (German People's Union) parties, and there are an additional 4,000 in other right-wing extremist organizations. From all of these groups a total of 10,000 right-wing extremists are categorized as violence-prone. All told, about 1,000 violent acts are committed by them annually, and most of them involve beating up and injuring foreigners or dark-skinned Germans. There are 1,000 right-wing extremist websites and several small publishing houses. The major medium of dissemination of such attitudes is right-wing extremist music.

Admittedly the distribution of those voting for the NPD and DVU parties varies strongly from region to region. In the September 18, 2005 elections for the German *Bundestag* they received 1.6% of the vote, but seen regionally the results range from 0.1% to levels that gain the NPD and DVU seats in local or state parliaments. In Sachsen the NPD party received 9.2% of the September 17, 2004 vote, or 12 parliamentary seats, and 7.3%, or 6 parliamentary seats, in the September 17, 2006 elections in Mecklenburg-Vorpommern. The DVU party received 6.1%, or 6 representatives, as a result of the election on September 19, 2004 in Brandenburg (the two parties never run against each other simultaneously).

What is it that right-wing extremists want? The report on constitutional protection concisely states and substantiates with numerous pieces of documentary evidence the following: "The right-wing extremist worldview is shaped by nationalistic and racist outlooks."[87] In addition there are two elements, which show right wing extremism to be a child of National Socialism. Those elements are political centralism and anti-Semitism. "As a general rule, right-wing extremism advocates an authoritarian political system, in which the state and the people, according to their notions of an ethnically homogeneous state as an alleged natural order, fuse into unity. According to this ideology of a 'national community,' the national leader should intuitively act according to the supposed uniform will of the people."[88] "Anti-Semitism remains the central ideological link between the diverse currents of right-wing extremism. This pertains above all to an anti-Semitism of insinuations, which, in addition to overt anti-Semitic agitation, has increased."[89] As evidence there is a statement by the NPD which is quoted: "The USA's foreign policy is made in Tel Aviv. In light of the agitation against Germany and the German people coming from Jewish circles, the USA, as an ally, is consequently more than dubious."[90]

Right-wing Extremism in Switzerland and Austria

Admittedly there are annual reports regarding extremism published annually in Switzerland and Austria. They are the "Report on the Internal Security of Switzerland" by the Service for Analysis and Prevention (DAP, or *Dienst für Analyse und Prävention*) of the Federal Office of Police and the constitutional protection report published by Austria's Federal Ministry for the Interior and its Federal Office for the Protection of the Constitution and Anti-Terrorism. However, in both countries it is not permitted to observe right-wing extremist organizations *per se*, as long as they are not demonstrating any violent activity. For this reason there are no precise numbers available from either of these countries with respect to the right-wing scene.

In Switzerland it is mostly only the violence-prone skinheads who are associated with right-wing extremism. The Federal Police estimate that

---

[87]   2007Annual Report of the Berlin Office for the Protection of the Constitution, Berlin: Federal Ministry of the Interior 2007, p. 46.

[88]   *Ibid.*

[89]   *Op. cit.*, p. 51.

[90]   *Op. cit.*, p. 81 with quotes from *Deutsche Stimme* No. 3/2007, p. 23.

there are 1,200 right-wing extremists and 800 sympathizers. Right-wing extremist parties in Switzerland are designated as 'nationally conservative' or 'conservative right.'

Right-wing parties in Austria are also legal, such as the FPÖ (Freedom Party of Austria, or *Freiheitliche Partei Österreichs*) which recently won an enormous proportion of the votes in federal elections. They are not monitored, and only neo-Nazism is criminally forbidden by law. In Austria it is also primarily the violence-prone skinhead scene that is considered right-wing extremist.

Excursus: The 'People' as a divine Order in Creation?

For many Christians 'the people,' in the sense of an ancestral community, possess a quality instilled by God that is found as well in areas such as family, church, work/commerce, and the state. However, while we find clear evidence in the Bible that God created the four named institutions, that he desires them, and that he confers authority upon them for certain tasks (e.g., Genesis 1:26-27, Romans 13:1-7, Ephesians 1), we do not find this anywhere with respect to the institution of 'the people.' Peoples emerge in the Bible, on the one hand, because people have children, but also because there is mixing via marriage, migration, and as a result of war.

If there is any sort of special people for Christians, then it is the Jews. God says that on no account did he choose Israel because it was something special (Deuteronomy 7:7-8). In addition, he furthermore did so in order to bless the world (Genesis 12:1-3) and not to harm it. And even for Israel what applied and applies is that it is not defined via biological ancestry but rather by its faith and its common history. Already in the Old Testament there were parts of ancestral line that broke away from the people of Israel, became 'lost' with respect to Israel, and developed their own history and culture (e.g., Esau and his descendants). Additionally, there were many a non-Jew who through conversion became full-fledged Jews (e.g., Moses' in-laws, Rahab the prostitute and her family, and Ruth).

What applies in light of the failure of many Christians at the time of National Socialism is the following: "The only response is – and Evangelical Christians have a holy responsibility to proclaim it without fear or partiality – is that no nation possesses the quality of salvation and that all peoples and all individuals are judged according to the exact same divine standard of righteousness . . ."[91]

---

[91] John Warwick Montgomery, *Christians in the Public Square*, Edmonton (Canada): Canadian Institute for Law, Theology, and Public Policy, 1996, p. 96.

There is no biblical justification for the classification of a racially and biologically defined people as its own authority structure and next to the state as a divine order of creation, one which is next to and delimited to the state. The state, as a general rule, always harbors at least some citizens of completely different ancestries. Along with Karl Barth I oppose the "elevation of the term 'people' to the level of theo-ethical main concepts,"[92] so that the people suddenly and allegedly become a 'divine order in creation,' such as the family. God gave the state the monopoly of power, the church the 'preaching monopoly,' and the family the 'child-rearing monopoly.' A biological 'people' has no authority over anyone. In fact, there is no such thing in the first place as a 'people.' Practically all the people of a nation are, historically viewed, a mixture of people. And to begin with, a mother tongue has nothing to do with racial affiliation. It is even often the case that numerous peoples speak the same language or that there are numerous languages found within one people.

---

[92] Karl Barth, *Die Kirchliche Dogmatik*, Study Edition vol. 19: Die Lehre von der Schöpfung III,4 §§ 52-54: Das Gebot Gottes des Schöpfers Part 1, Zürich 1993 (1951), p. 345.

Internet Links and Bibliography

The following order is maintained below:

Weblinks (according to importance)
Articles in the web
English books and articles
German books and articles

Racism – Science

In English:

Michael *Barkun*, Religion and the Racist Right: The Origins of the Christian Identity Movement, North Carolina: The University of North Carolina Press 1997

Joe R. *Feagin*, Systemic Racism: A Theory of Oppression, New York Routledge 2006

Alana *Lentin*, Racism: A Beginner's Guide, Oxford: One World 2008

Albert *Memmi*, Racism, Minneapolis (MI): University of Minnesota Press 2000

Ali *Rattansi*, Racism: A Very Short Introduction, Oxford: Oxford University Press 2009

Bettina *Wohlgemuth*, Racism in the 21st century – How Everybody Can Make a Difference, Saarbrücken: Verlag Dr. Müller 2007

In German:

www.comlink.de/cl-hh/m.blumentritt/agr52s.htm

http://www.ekr-cfr.ch/themen/00023/index.html?lang=de

Mathias *Bös*, Rasse und Ethnizität: Zur Problemgeschichte zweier Begriffe in der amerikanischen Soziologie, Wiesbaden: Verlag für Sozialwissenschaften 2005

Maureen Maisha *Eggers* u. a. (Hg.), Mythen, Masken und Subjekte: Kritische Weißseinsforschung in Deutschland, Münster: Lit 2005

Wulf D. *Hund,* Negative Vergesellschaftung, Münster: Verlag Westfälisches Dampfboot 2006

Wulf D. *Hund,* Rassismus: Die soziale Konstruktion natürlicher Ungleichheit, Münster: Verlag Westfälisches Dampfboot 1999

Wulf D. *Hund,* Rassismus, Bielefeld: Transcript-Verlag 2007

Paul *Jobst*, Das „Tier"-Konstrukt und die Geburt des Rassismus: Zur kulturellen Gegenwart eines vernichtenden Arguments, Münster: Unrast-Verlag 2004

Wolfgang *Wippermann*, Rassenwahn und Teufelsglaube, Berlin: Frank & Timme 2005

Johannes *Zerger*, Was ist Rassismus? Göttingen: Lamuv 1997

Genetics, Race, and Racism

In English:

Declaration of Schlaining against racism, violence and discrimination. Vienna: The Austrian Commission for UNESCO, 1995: www.aspr.ac.at/publications/declar~1.pdf

www.scinexx.de/wissen-aktuell-7846-2008-02-22.html: „Karte enthüllt genetische Vielfalt der Völker" (Springer-Verlag)

www.gene.ch/genpost/2005/Jul-Dec/msg00203.html: „Atlas der genetischen Vielfalt der Menschen"

Find A list of scientific articles on genetics in Dave *Unander*, Shattering the Myth of Race: Genetic Realities and Biblical Truths, Valley Forge: Judson Press 2000, pp. 119-127

Luigi Luca *Cavalli-Sforza* et al, The History and Geography of Human Genes, Princeton: Princeton University Press 1994

Luigi Luca *Cavalli-Sforza*, Genes, Peoples, and Languages, Berkeley (CA): Univ. of California Press 2001

Luigi Luca *Cavalli-Sforza*, The Great Human Diasporas: The History of Diversity and Evolution, Reading (MA): Addison-Wesley 1995

Scientific Criticism of the term "Race" or Division by Race

In English:

http://en.wikipedia.org/wiki/Race_(classification_of_humans)

Declaration on Race and Racial Prejudice. UNESCO 27/11/1978. http://www.unesco.org/webworld/peace_library/UNESCO/HRIGHTS/107-116.htm

Wulf D. *Hund*, "Inclusion and Exclusion: Dimensions of Racism", Wiener Zeitschrift zur Geschichte der Neuzeit, 3 (2003) 1: 1-19; http://www.wiso.uni-hamburg.de/fileadmin/wiso_dwp_soz/Hund/wr_zeitsch_art_hund.pdf

Ulrich *Kattmann*, Race, genes, and racism, Proceedings of the first conference on Applied Interculturality Research, Graz 2010, http://www.uni-graz.at/fAIR/cAIR10/text/procs/Kattmann_cAIR10.pdf

Stephen Jay *Gould*, Mismeasure of Man, New York: Norton 1981-1; 2008-2

Joseph *Graves*, The Race Myth. New York: Dutton 2004

Dinesh *D'Souza*, The End of Racism, New York: Free Press 1997

Audrey *Smedley*, Brian D. *Smedley*. "Race as Biology is Fiction, Racism as a Social Problem is Real." American Psychologist 60 (2005): 16-26

Barbara *Trepagnier,* Silent Racism: How Well-Meaning White People Perpetuate the Racial Divide, Boulder & London: Paradigm Publishers 2006

Dave *Unander*, Shattering the Myth of Race: Genetic Realities and Biblical Truths, Valley Forge: Judson Press 2000

In German:

Ulrich *Kattmann*, „Rassismus, Biologie und Rassenlehre", in: www.shoa.de/content/view/368/96/

Frank *Böckelmann*, Die Gelben, die Schwarzen, die Weißen, Frankfurt: Eichborn 1999

Walter *Demel*, „Wie die Chinesen gelb wurden: Ein Beitrag zur Frühgeschichte der Rassentheorien", in: *Historische Zeitschrift* 255 (1992), pp. 625-666

Stephen Jay *Gould*, „Warum wir menschliche Rassen nicht benennen sollten", in: *Gould*, Darwin nach Darwin, Frankfurt: Ullstein 1984, pp. 195-200

Wolfram *Henn*, Warum Frauen nicht schwach, Schwarze nicht dumm und Behinderte nicht arm dran sind: Der Mythos von den guten Genen, Freiburg: Herder 2004

Ulrich *Kattmann*, „Menschenrassen", in: Lexikon der Biologie. Bd. 9, Heidelberg: Spektrum 2002, pp. 170-177

Ulrich *Kattmann*, „Rassismus", in: Lexikon der Biologie. Bd. 11, Heidelberg: Spektrum 2003, pp. 423-424

Heidrun *Kaupen-Haas*/Christian *Saller*, Wissenschaftlicher Rassismus: Analysen einer Kontinuität in den Human-Naturwissenschaften, Frankfurt: Campus 1999

Christian *Schüller*/Petrus *van der Let*, Rasse Mensch: Jeder Mensch ein Mischling, Aschaffenburg: Alibri 1999

IQ and "Race"

In English:

http://de.wikipedia.org/wiki/The_Bell_Curve

Stephen Jay *Gould*, Mismeasure of Man, New York: Norton 1981-1; 2008-2

In German:

Gunnar *Heinsohn*, „Die Crux mit der Intelligenz", in: *Die Welt* vom 26.11.2007, pp. 7 (= www.welt.de/wissenschaft/article1400104/Die_Crux_mit_der_Intelligenz.html)

Michael *Shermer* u. a., Argumente und Kritik: Skeptisches Jahrbuch 1997 Aschaffenburg: Alibri 1996 (vier Artikel gegen „The Bell Curve")

Christian Voices against Racism and the Term 'Race'

In English:

Jefferson D. *Edwards*, Purging Racism from Christianity, Grand Rapids: Zondervan 1996

Garth *Lean*, God's politician: William Wilberforce's Struggle, Colorado Springs: Helmers & Howard 1987

Eric *Metaxas*, Amazing Grace: William Wilberforce and the Heroic Campaign to End Slavery, New York: HarperCollins 2007

John *Stott*, Human Rights & Human Wrongs, Grand Rapids (MI): Baker 1999, chapter on racism

Christopher Leslie *Brown*, Moral Capital: Foundations of British Abolitionism, Chapel Hill (NC): Univ. of North Carolina Press 2006

Dave *Unander*, Shattering the Myth of Race: Genetic Realities and Biblical Truths, Valley Forge: Judson Press 2000

In German:

Peter *Beyerhaus*, Rassismus, seine evangeliumsgemäße Überwindung, Bad Liebenzell: VLM 1972 = Peter Beyerhaus. Krise und Neuaufbruch der Weltmission, Bad Liebenzell: VLM 1987, pp. 123-145

Thomas *Schirrmacher*, Multikulturelle Gesellschaft, Holzgerlingen: Hänssler 2007

'Race' – older, outdated Presentations

In English:

Henry Neville *Hutchinson*, The Living Races of Mankind, Hutchinson: SL 1901

John R. P. *McKenzie*, The Uncivilized Races of Men in all Countries of the World ..., Delhi (India): Daya Publ. House 1986

In German:

Gerhard *Heberer* u.a. (Hg.), Anthropologie: Das Fischer Lexikon, Frankfurt: Fischer 1970, esp. articles „Rasse", „Rassengeschichte", „Rassenpsychologie"

Georg *Kenntner*, Rassen aus Erbe und Umwelt, Berlin: Safari-Verlag 1975

Neo-Nazi Justification of 'Racial Doctrine'

In English:

Mattias *Gardell*, Gods of the Blood: The Pagan Revival and White Separatism, Durham: Duke University Press 2003

Nicholas *Goodrick-Clark*. Black Sun: Aryan Cults, Esoteric Nazism and the Politics of Identity. New York: New York University Press 2002

Heléne *Lööw*, From National Socialism to Militant Racism: The Swedish Racist Underground in the 1990s, Tel Aviv: Project for the Study of Anti-Semitism 1996

Chester L. *Quarles*, Christian Identity: The Aryan American Bloodline Religion, Jefferson (NC): McFarland 2004

Neo-Nazi-Literature in German:

www.npd.de, dann „Inhalte", dann „Politisches Lexikon"

Johannes P. *Ney*, Reizwort Rasse, Riesa: Deutsche Stimme Verlag 2000

Hans F. K. *Günther*/Jürgen *Spanuth*, Die nordische Rasse bei den Indogermanen Asiens, Pähl: Verlag Hohe Warte 1982

Racism – History

In English:

http://en.wikipedia.org/wiki/Racism

Theodore *Allen*, The Invention of the White Race: 2 vol., London: Verso 1997

Elazar *Barkan*, The Retreat of Scientific Racism: Changing Concepts of Race in Britain and the United States, Cambridge: Cambridge University Press 2000

George M. *Fredrickson*, Racism: A Short History, Princeton/Oxford: Princeton University Press 2002

Léon *Poliakov*, The Arian Myth, London: Chatto, Heinemann 1974

Ann Laura *Stoler*, „Racial Histories and Their Regimes of Truth", Political Power and Social Theory 11 (1997): 183-206

Andrew *Valls* (Hg.), Race and Racism in Modern Philosophy, Ithaca: Cornell University Press 2005

In German:

http://de.wikipedia.org/wiki/Rassentheorien

Werner *Conze*/Antje *Sommer*, „Rasse", in: Otto *Brunner*/Werner *Conze*/Reinhart *Koselleck* (Hg.), Geschichtliche Grundbegriffe. Historisches Lexikon zur politisch-sozialen Sprache in Deutschland, Bd. 5, Stuttgart: Klett-Cotta 2004, pp. 135-178

Christian *Delacampagne*, Die Geschichte des Rassismus, Düsseldorf: Artemis & Winkler 2005

Imanuel *Geiss*, Geschichte des Rassismus, Frankfurt: Suhrkamp 1993

Christian *Geulen*, Geschichte des Rassismus, München: C. H. Beck 2007

George L. *Mosse*, Die Geschichte des Rassismus in Europa, Frankfurt: Fischer 2006

Léon *Poliakov* / Christian *Delacampagne* / Patrick *Girard*, Rassismus: Über Fremdenfeindlichkeit und Rassenwahn, Hamburg: Luchterhand 1992

Karin *Priester*, Rassismus – Eine Sozialgeschichte, Leipzig: Reclam 2003

Anti-Semitism and Genocide of Jews in the Third Reich

In English:

Doris L. *Bergen*, War and Genocide: A Concise History of the Holocaust, Lanham (MD): Rowman & Littlefield 2002

Eric *Ehrenreich*, The Nazi Ancestral Proof: Genealogy, Racial Science, and the Final Solution, Indiana University Press, Bloomington (IN) 2007

William *Samelson*, Warning and hope: The Nazi Murder of European Jewry. London: Vallentine Mitchell 2003

Robert M. *Spector*, World Without Civilization: Mass Murder and the Holocaust, Lanham (MD), Oxford: University Press of America 2005

In German:

Wolfgang *Benz* (Hg.), Dimension des Völkermords: Die Zahl der jüdischen Opfer des Nationalsozialismus, München: dtv 1996

Wolfgang *Benz* (Hg.), Der Hass gegen die Juden: Dimensionen und Formen des Antisemitismus, Berlin: Metropol 2008

Werner *Bergmann*, Geschichte des Antisemitismus, München: C. H. Beck 2006-3rd

Hubert *Cancik*/Uwe *Puschner* (Hg.), Antisemitismus, Paganismus, Völkische Religion, München: K.G. Saur 2004

Matthias *Küntzel*, Islamischer Antisemitismus und deutsche Politik, Münster: Lit 2007

Manfred *Lahnstein*, Die offene Wunde: Antisemitismus als Schicksal? Bergisch Gladbach: Bastei Lübbe 2007

Jürgen *Matthäus*/Klaus-Michael *Mallmann* (Hg.), Deutsche, Juden, Völkermord. Der Holocaust in Geschichte und Gegenwart, Darmstadt: Wissenschaftliche Buchgesellschaft 2006

Gerald *Messadié*, Verfolgt und auserwählt: Die lange Geschichte des Antisemitismus, München: Piper 2001

Dieter *Pohl*, Verfolgung und Massenmord in der NS-Zeit 1933-1945, Darmstadt: Wissenschaftliche Buchgesellschaft 2003

Léon *Poliakov*, Geschichte des Antisemitismus in 8 Bänden, Worms: Heintz Verlag 1977-1988

Lars *Rensmann*/Julius H. *Schoeps* (Hg.), Feindbild Judentum: Antisemitismus in Europa, Berlin: Verlag für Berlin-Brandenburg 2008

Peter *Waldbauer*, Lexikon der antisemitischen Klischees: Antijüdische Vorurteile und ihre historische Entstehung, Murnau am Staffelsee: Mankau 2007

The Racism of National Socialism

In English:

Stefan *Kühl*, The Nazi Connection Eugenics, American Racism, and German National Socialism, New York: Oxford Univ. Press 1994

Allan *Mitchell* (ed.), The Nazi Revolution: Hitler's dictatorship and the German nation, Boston: Houghton Mifflin 1997

Gretchen E. *Schafft*, From Racism to Genocide: Anthropology in the Third Reich, Urbana: University of Illinois Press 2004

Richard *Weikart*, From Darwin to Hitler: Evolutionary ethics, eugenics, and racism in Germany, Basingstoke (USA): Palgrave Macmillan 2005

In German:

Peter E. *Becker*, Wege ins Dritte Reich, Teil 2: Sozialdarwinismus, Rassismus, Antisemitismus, Stuttgart: Thieme 1990

Wolfgang *Benz* (Hg.), Legenden, Lügen, Vorurteile: Ein Wörterbuch zur Zeitgeschichte, München: dtv 1993-4th

Uwe *Puschner*, „Grundzüge völkischer Rassenideologie", in: Achim *Leube* (Hg.), Prähistorie und Nationalsozialismus, Heidelberg: Wissenschaftsverlag der Autoren 2002, pp. 49-72

Uwe *Puschner*, „Germanenideologie und völkische Weltanschauung". in: Heinrich *Beck* u. a. (Hg.), Zur Geschichte der Gleichung „germanisch-deutsch", Berlin: de Gruyter 2004, pp. 103-130

Thomas *Schirrmacher*, Hitlers Kriegsreligion: Die Verankerung der Weltanschauung Hitlers in seiner religiösen Begrifflichkeit und seinem Gottesbild, 2 vol., Bonn: VKW 2007

Rainer *Zitelmann*, Hitler: Selbstverständnis eines Revolutionärs, Stuttgart: Klett-Cotta 1989-2nd

Genocide in general

In English:

http://de.wikipedia.org/wiki/Genozid

Journal of Genocide Research, London (since 1999)

Robert *Gellately* (ed.), The Specter of Genocide: Mass Murder in Historical Perspective, Cambridge: Cambridge Univ. Press 2010

Leonard S. *Newman*, Ralph *Erber* (ed.), Understanding Genocide: The Social Psychology of the Holocaust, Oxford: Oxford University Press 2002

Samuel *Totten*/Paul R. *Bartrop*, Dictionary of Genocide. 2 vol., West-port: Greenwood Press 2008

In German:

www.gfbv.de (Gesellschaft für bedrohte Völker)

www.gfbv.de/pogrome.php (Journal „Pogrom")

Richard *Albrecht*, Genozidpolitik im 20. Jahrhundert, 3 Bde., Aachen: Shaker 2006

Boris *Barth*, Genozid. Völkermord im 20. Jahrhundert. Geschichte, Theorien, Kontroversen, München: Beck 2006

Thoralf *Klein*/Frank *Schumacher* (Hg.), Kolonialkriege – Militärische Gewalt im Zeichen des Imperialismus, Hamburg: Hamburger Edition 2005

William A. *Schabas*, Genozid im Völkerrecht, Hamburg: Hamburger Edition 2003

Frank *Selbmann*, Der Tatbestand des Genozids im Völkerstrafrecht, Leipzig: Leipziger Universitätsverlag 2002

Jürgen *Zimmerer*/Joachim *Zeller* (Hg.), Völkermord in Deutsch-Südwestafrika: Der Kolonialkrieg (1904-1908) in Namibia und seine Folgen, Berlin: Christoph Links Verlag 2003

Slavery

In English:

www.antislavery.org

Keith *Bradley*, Paul *Cartledge*, The Cambridge World History of Slavery, New York: Cambridge Univ. Press 2009

Indrani *Chatterjee*, Richard M. *Eaton*, Slavery & South Asian History, Bloomington(IN): Indiana University Press 2006

Seymour *Drescher*, Abolition: A History of Slavery and Antislavery, Cambridge: Cambridge University Press 2009

Seymour *Drescher* (ed.), A Historical Guide to World Slavery, New York: Oxford Univ. Press 2010

In German:

Christian *Delacampagne*, Die Geschichte der Sklaverei, Darmstadt: Wissenschaftliche Buchgesellschaft 2004

Susanne *Everett*, Geschichte der Sklaverei, Augsburg: Bechtermünz 1998

Harm *Mögenburg*/Heinz-Peter *Rauckes*, Sklaverei und Dreieckshandel: Menschen als Ware, Frankfurt: Diesterweg 1988

See next rubric for slavery in the USA

USA

In English:

Edward E. *Baptist*, Stephanie M. H. *Camp,* New Studies in the History of American Slavery, Athens (GE): University of Georgia Press 2006

Dinesh *D'Souza*, The End of Racism, New York: Simon & Schuster 1995

John Hope *Franklin*/ Evelyn Brooks, *Higginbotham*, From Slavery to Freedom: A History of African Americans, New York: McGraw-Hill 2011

Jessie *Daniels*, White Lies: Race, Class, Gender and Sexuality in White Supremacist Discourse, New York: Routledge 1997

Jessie *Daniels*, Cyber Racism: White Supremacy Online and the New Attack on Civil Rights, Lanham (MD): Rowman & Littlefield 2009

Joe R. *Feagin*, Racist America: Roots, Current Realities, and Future Reparations, New York: Routledge 2009-2

Audrey *Smedley*, Race in North America: Origins and Evolution of a World View. Boulder, (CO): Westview 2007

Michael *Vorenberg*, Final Freedom: The Civil War, the Abolition of Slavery, and the Thirteenth Amendment, Cambridge: Cambridge University Press 2001

Howard *Winant*, The New Politics of Race, Boulder (CO): Westview 2004

Howard *Winant*, Michael *Omi*, Racial Formation in The United States, New York: Routeledge 1994-2nd

In German:

Richard *Herzinger*, „Obamas Problem ist nicht der Rassismus", in: *Die Welt* vom 11.6.2008 (= www.welt.de/politik/article2088714/Obamas_Problem_ist_nicht_der_Rassismus.html)

Oliver *Demny*, Rassismus in den USA: Historie und Analyse einer Rassenkonstruktion, Münster: Unrast-Verlag 2001

Jochen *Meissner* u. a., Schwarzes Amerika: Eine Geschichte der Sklaverei, München: C.H. Beck 2008

South Africa

In English:

William *Beinart*, Saul *Dubow* (Hg.), Segregation and Apartheid in Twentieth-Century South-Africa, London: Routledge 1995

In German:

Lutz *Brinkmann*, Sandown – weiße Kindheit im Apartheidsstaat, Schriesheim: Dunkelblau Verlag 2004

Pumla *Gobodo-Madikizela*, Das Erbe der Apartheid – Trauma, Erinnerung, Versöhnung, Opladen: Verlag Barbara Budrich 2006

Nelson *Mandela*, Der lange Weg zur Freiheit: Autobiographie, Frankfurt: S. Fischer 1994 (viele weitere Auflagen)

Gypsies

In English:

http://en.wikipedia.org/wiki/Romani_people

Isabel *Fonseca*, Bury me Standing: The Gypsies and their Journey, New York: A.A. Knopf 1995

David *Gresham* u. a., „Origins and Divergence of the Roma (Gypsies)", in: *American Journal of Human Genetics* 69 (2001), pp. 1314-1331

In German:

Rajko *Djurić* u. a., Ohne Heim – ohne Grab: Die Geschichte der Roma und Sinti, Berlin: Aufbau-Verlag 2002

Reimer *Gronemeyer*/Georgia A. *Rakelmann*, Die Zigeuner, Köln: DuMont 1988

Joachim S. *Hohmann*, Geschichte der Zigeunerverfolgung in Deutschland, Frankfurt: Campus 1988

Leo *Lucassen*, Zigeuner: Die Geschichte eines polizeilichen Ordnungsbegriffes in Deutschland 1700–1945, Köln: Böhlau Verlag 1996

Romani *Rose* (Hg.), Der nationalsozialistische Völkermord an den Sinti und Roma, Heidelberg: Dokumentations- und Kulturzentrum Deutscher Sinti und Roma 1995

Racism in other Countries

In English:

http://en.wikipedia.org/wiki/Armenian_Genocide

http://en.wikipedia.org/wiki/War_in_Darfur

Northern Ireland: http://en.wikipedia.org/wiki/The_Troubles

S. M. *Michael,* ed., Dalits in Modern India: Vision and Values, London: Sage 2007-2

Joseph *D'souza*, Dalit Freedom, Centennial: Dalit Freedom Network 2006 (India)

Artem *Ohandjanian*, ed., The Armenian Genocide, 2 vol., Munich: Institute für Armenische Fragen 1988

Samuel *Totten*/Eric *Markusen* (Hg.), Genocide in Darfur: Investigating the Atrocities in the Sudan, New York: Routledge 2006

Alex *de Waal*/Julie *Flient*, Darfur: A Short History of a Long War, London: Zed Books 2006

France Winddance *Twine*, Racism in a Racial Democracy: The Maintenance of White Supremacy in Brazil, New York: Rutgers University Press 1977

In German:

Stéphane *Courtois*, Das Schwarzbuch des Kommunismus: Unterdrückung, Verbrechen und Terror, München: Piper 1998

Alison *Des Forges*, Kein Zeuge darf überleben: Der Genozid in Ruanda, Hamburg: Hamburger Edition 2002

Gerhard *Leitner*, Die Aborigines Australiens, München: C.H. Beck 2006

Peter *Martin*, Schwarze Teufel, edle Mohren: Afrikaner in Bewußtsein und Geschichte der Deutschen, Hamburg: Junius 2001

Frank *Otto*, Der Nordirlandkonflikt, München: C.H. Beck 2005

Gérard *Prunier*, Darfur. Der „uneindeutige" Genozid, Hamburg: Hamburger Edition 2007

Thilo *Thielke*, Krieg im Lande des Mahdi: Darfur und der Zerfall Sudans, Essen: Magnus Verlag 2006

Brigitte *Voykowitsch*, Dalits – Die Unberührbaren in Indien, Wien: Verlag Der Apfel 2006

Ethnology – Cultural Anthropology – Peoples of the World

In English:

Jack David *Eller*, Cultural Anthropology, New York: Routledge 2009

Paul G. *Hiebert*, Cultural Anthropology, Grand Rapids: Baker 1986[3rd]

Francis *Huxley*, Peoples of the World in Colour, London: Blandford Press 1975

Roger M. *Keesing*/Andrew J. *Strathern*, Cultural Anthropology, Fort Worth: Harcourt Brace College Publishers 1998-3rd

Thomas *Schirrmacher,* "Cannibalism and Human Sacrifice Vindicated?" in: *Christianity and Society* 10 (2000) 1, pp. 11-17 and 2, pp. 4-9

Secretariat of the Permanent Forum on Indigenous Issues, State of the World's Indigenous Peoples, New York: United Nations 2009

In German:

Christoph *Antweiler*, Grundpositionen interkultureller Ethnologie, Nordhausen: Bautz 2007

Heike *Barnitzke*, Die Welt in der wir leben, München: Kunth 2008

Edward *Evans-Pritchard* (Hg.), Bild der Völker: Die Brockhaus-Völkerkunde in 10 Bänden, Wiesbaden: Brockhaus 1974-1977

Mirella *Ferrera*, Völker der Welt, Köln: Karl Müller 2003

Roland *Girtler*, Kulturanthropologie: Eine Einführung, Münster: Lit 2006

Walter *Hirschberg* u. a., Wörterbuch der Völkerkunde, Berlin: Reimer 2005-2nd

Lothar *Käser*, Fremde Kulturen: Eine Einführung in die Ethnologie, Bad Liebenzell: VLM 2005-3rd

Klemens *Ludwig*, Bedrohte Völker: Nationale und religiöse Minderheiten, München: C.H. Beck 1994-3rd

Klemens *Ludwig*, Ethnische Minderheiten in Europa: Ein Lexikon, München: C.H. Beck 1995

Thomas *Schirrmacher*, Multikulturelle Gesellschaft: Chancen und Gefahren, Holzgerlingen: Hänssler 2006

Thomas *Schirrmacher*, Scham- oder Schuldgefühl? Die christliche Botschaft angesichts von schuld- und schamorientierten Gewissen und Kulturen, Bonn: VKW 2005

Thomas *Schirrmacher*, Völker – Drogen – Kannibalismus: Ethnologische und länderkundliche Beiträge, Bonn: VKW 1997

Thomas *Schirrmacher*/Klaus W. *Müller* (Hg.), Scham- und Schuldorientierung in der Diskussion: Kulturanthropologische, missiologische und theologische Einsichten, Bonn: VKW und Nürnberg: VTR 2006

Cornelia *Schmalz-Jacobsen*/Georg *Hansen* (Hg.), Kleines Lexikon der ethnischen Minderheiten in Deutschland, Bonn: Bundeszentrale für Politische Bildung 1997

Willi *Stegner* (Hg.), Taschenatlas Völker und Sprachen, Gotha: Klett-Perthes 2006

Meic *Stephens*, Minderheiten in Westeuropa, Husum: Matthiesen 1979

Herbert *Tischner* (Hg.), Völkerkunde: Das Fischer Lexikon, Frankfurt: Fischer 1959

Frank Robert *Vivelo*, Handbuch der Kulturanthropologie, Stuttgart: Klett-Cotta 1995-2nd

Current Day Opposition to Racism in Germany, Austria, and Switzerland

International – in English:

http://www.racismreview.com/blog/

http://www.antiracismandhate.com/

International: www.humanrightsfirst.org/discrimination/ (2008 Hate Crime Survey)

In German speaking countries – in German:

Germany: http://aric-nrw.de (Anti-Rassismus-Informations-Centrum)

Germany: http://idaev.de und www.ida-nrw.de (Informations- und Dokumentationszentrum für Antirassismusarbeit e. V. [IDA])

Switzerland: www.ekr-cfr.ch (Eidgenössische Kommission gegen Rassismus)

Switzerland: Beratungsnetz für Rassismusopfer: http://d102352.u28.netvs.ch/bfr/index.asp

Switzerland: Aktuelle Vorfälle und Rechtsfälle: www.humanrights.ch/home/?idcat=128 und www.gra.ch

Katrin *Monen*, Das Verbot der Diskriminierung: Eine Untersuchung aufgrund der Rasse, des Geschlechts und der sexuellen Identität im deutschen und U.S.-amerikanischen Privatrecht (Dissertation), Baden-Baden: Nomos 2008, „Rasse" esp. pp. 89ff

Right-Wing Extremism today

http://en.wikipedia.org/wiki/Category:White_supremacy

http://en.wikipedia.org/wiki/White_supremacy

In German Speaking Countries – in German:

Deutschland: Verfassungsschutzbericht 2007, Berlin: Bundesministerium des Innern 2007, Download unter www.verfassungsschutz.de/de/publikationen/verfassungsschutzbericht/vsbericht_2007/

Deutschland: Bundesamt für Verfassungsschutz, Verfassungsschutz gegen Rechtsextremismus, Berlin 2008, http://www.verfassungsschutz.de/download/de/publikationen/pb_rechtsextremismus/broschuere_2_0807_vs_gegen_rechtsextrem/broschuere_0807_vs_gegen_rechtsextrem.pdf

Verfassungsschutzbericht des Landes Nordrhein-Westfalen über das Jahr 2007, Düsseldorf: Innenministerium des Landes NRW 2008, pp. 45-88, Download unter www.im.nrw.de/sch/doks/vs/aktuell.pdf

Schweiz: Bericht zur Inneren Sicherheit: www.fedpol.admin.ch/fedpol/de/home/dokumentation/berichte.html und www.fedpol.admin.ch/fedpol/de/home/dokumentation/berichte/extremismus.html

Österreich: Bundesministerium für Inneres/Bundesamt für Verfassungsschutz und Terrorismusbekämpfung (Hg.), Verfassungsschutzbericht 2007, www.bmi.gv.at/downloadarea/staatsschutz/BVT%20VSB%202007%2020070724%20Onlineversion.pdf

Österreich: http://www.inprekorr.de/341-oest.htm (zur Geschichte des Rechtsextremismus in Österreich)

Jahrbuch Extremismus & Demokratie 20 (2008) und frühere Jahrgänge, auch mit Länderberichten zu Deutschland, Österreich, Schweiz

Kai *Arzheimer*, Die Wähler der extremen Rechten 1980–2002, Wiesbaden: Verlag für Sozialwissenschaften 2008 (Deutschland)

Elmar *Brähler*/Oliver *Decker*, Rechtsextremismus in Deutschland, Leipzig: Universität Leipzig 2004, www.uni-leipzig.de/~medpsy/pdf/rechtsextremismus_230605.pdf

Oliver *Decker* u. a., Ein Blick in die Mitte: Zur Entstehung rechts-extremer und demokratischer Einstellungen in Deutschland, Berlin: Fried-rich-Ebert-Stiftung 2008, Download unter http://library.fes.de/pdf-files/do/05433.pdf, Kurzfassung: www.fes.de/rechtsextremismus/inhalt/studie.htm (Deutschland)

Viola B. *Georgi* u. a. (Hg.), Strategien gegen Rechtsextremismus, 2 vol., Gütersloh: Bertelsmann-Stiftung 2005

Thomas *Grumke*/Bernd *Wagner* (Hg.), Handbuch Rechtsradikalismus, Opladen: Leske + Budrich 2002

Andreas *Klärner*/Michael *Kohlstruck* (Hg.), Moderner Rechtsextre-mismus in Deutschland, Hamburg: Hamburger Edition 2006

Richard *Meisel*, Rechtsextremismus, die Neue Rechte und aktuelle rechtsextreme Strömungen, Wien: Verband Österreichischer Gewerk-schaftlicher Bildung 2006, Download unter www.voegb.at/bildungsangebote/skripten/pzg/PZG-05B.pdf (Österreich)

Armin *Pfahl-Traughber*, Rechtsextremismus in der Bundesrepublik, München: C.H. Beck 2006-4th

Helmut *Reinalter* u. a. (Hg.), Das Weltbild des Rechtsextremismus, Innsbruck: StudienVerlag 1998

Dehumanizing Caste System

Overcoming an Indian Form of Racism

Rev. Dr. Richard Howell, India
General Secretary of the Evangelical Fellowship of India
General Secretary of the Asian Evangelical Alliance

In 1963 Martin Luther King, Jr. eloquently shared his vision of the future. His faith-filled dream of freedom, dignity, and justice continues to inspire with courageous hope all who hear his words. "I have a dream that one day this nation will rise up and live out the true meaning of its creed: We hold these truths to be self-evident, that all men are created equal, that they are endowed by their Creator with certain unalienable Rights that among these are Life, Liberty and the pursuit of Happiness." King Jr. fought racism in America.

In 1924 B.R. Ambedkar (Ph.D., Economics, Columbia University, and D.Sc., London University), a Dalit, returned to India. He received no merit nor was any honour accorded to him. Instead, he was exposed to ugly opposition, relentless intellectual criticism, and caste-bound cultural humiliations. On Christmas Day 1927, Dr. Ambedkar publicly burned Manu Smiriti, the most sacred and basic document Brahmins used to justify caste and ascribe untouchability. Says Manu, the ancient lawgiver of brahmanical tradition, "When a Brahman is born, he springs to light above the world; he is the chief of all creatures, entitled by eminence of birth to the wealth of the world" (Manusmriti.I.98-100). Dr. Ambedkar fought casteism in India.

"Had Ambedkar not learned English, he would not have gone abroad," said Eash Kumar Gangania, "and had he not gone abroad, he would not have become Babasaheb for us." Ambedkar became the Father of the Indian Constitution. Gangania, a teacher from Delhi, was speaking to 1,500 Dalits in a remote village of Bankagaon, in UP. The crowd was rapt as Gangania added that it all happened "because Ambedkar learned English," finally ending with a powerful and surprising message: "If you learn English, you, too, can scale the heights Babasaheb did." Gangania's speech came on a special occasion, 30 April 2010, the day Bankagaon's Dalits pledged to learn the English language as well as worship it as a goddess. It was the day they laid the foundations of a temple dedicated to "English, the

Dalit Goddess." The Dalits' quest for English is their attempt to find a voice. It has all the ingredients of an epic struggle. This goddess may not join the Hindu pantheon of 330 million, but it could usher in an era of cultural rejuvenation for Dalits.[1]

The caste system is based on the principle of discrimination and inequality. It is one of the most rigid and institutionalised brutalities of Hindu society. While the agenda for political freedom of India from British rule was achieved in 1947, the freedom to emancipate the masses from perpetual exploitation and oppression remains to be won. Phule, Ambedkar, and Periyar continued to advocate that "a society divided by social oppression could not constitute a genuine nation."[2]

Ontological Basis for Caste

The *Purusha Sukta* is an important part of the Rig-Veda (10.7.90.1-16). This hymn is recited in almost all Vedic rituals and ceremonies. According to this hymn, from the body of Brahma come the four main categories of Hindu society, namely the four *varnas* or castes: From His face (or the mouth) came the *Brahmans,* the priests. From His two arms came the *kshatriyas,* the warrior. From His two thighs came the *vaishyas*, the businessman. From His two feet came the *shudras,* the servants. Caste system thus has ontological value.

The untouchables are born from outside the body of the Creator, almost a different species from Brahma's children. Their entry into the divine body would be as unthinkable as the entry of an animal. The word "Dalit," meaning "crushed underfoot" or "broken into pieces," is the contemporary version of the word "Untouchable."

The Ritual Purity and Pollution

Many status differences in Indian society are expressed in terms of ritual purity and pollution. Reflecting on the opposition between "the pure and the impure" in his classic exposition *Homo Hierarchicus,* Louis Dumont has argued that this binary opposition is the ideological principal and the essence of the caste system.[3] Notions of purity and pollution are extremely complex and vary greatly among different castes, religious groups, and regions. However, broadly speaking, high status is associated with purity

---

[1]   D Shyam Babu, "D is for Dalits and E is for the English Goddess," *The Times of India,* May 9, 2010.

[2]   Gail Omvedit, *Dalit and the Democratic Revolution: Dr Ambedkar and the Dalit Movement in Colonial India,* Delhi: Sage, 1994.

[3]   Louis Dumont. *Homo Hierarchius.* Delhi: Vikas Publications, 1970, pp.33-64.

and low status with pollution. Some kinds of purity are inherent, or inborn; for example, gold is purer than copper by its very nature and, similarly, a member of a high-ranking Brahman, or priestly, caste is born with more inherent purity than is a member of a low-ranking Dalit. Unless the Brahman defiles himself in some extraordinary way, throughout his life he will always be purer than a Dalit. Other kinds of purity are more transitory – a Brahman who has just taken a bath is more ritually pure than is a Brahman who has not bathed for a day. This situation could easily reverse itself temporarily, depending on bath schedules, participation in polluting activities, or contact with temporarily polluting substances.

Purity is associated with ritual cleanliness – daily bathing in flowing water, dressing in properly laundered clothes of approved materials, eating only the foods appropriate for one's caste, refraining from physical contact with people of lower rank, and avoiding involvement with ritually impure substances. The latter include body wastes and excretions, most especially those of another adult person. Contact with the products of death or violence is typically polluting and threatening to ritual purity.

A Brahman born of proper Brahman parents retains his inherent purity if he bathes and dresses himself properly, adheres to a vegetarian diet, eats meals prepared only by persons of appropriate rank, and keeps his person away from the bodily exuviate of others (except for necessary contact with the secretions of family infants and small children). If a Brahman happens to come into bodily contact with a polluting substance, he can remove this pollution by bathing and changing his clothing. However, if he were to eat meat or commit other transgressions of the rigid dietary codes of his particular caste, he would be considered more deeply polluted and would have to undergo various purifying rites and payment of fines imposed by his caste council in order to restore his inherent purity.

In sharp contrast to the purity of a Brahman, a Dalit born of Dalit parents is considered to be born inherently polluted. Touching his body is polluting to those higher on the caste hierarchy than he, and they will shrink from his touch, whether or not he has bathed recently. Dalits are associated with the traditional occupation of cleaning human feces from latrines and sweeping public lanes of all kinds of dirt. Traditionally, Dalits remove these polluting materials in baskets carried atop the head and dumped out in a garbage pile at the edge of the village or neighbourhood. The involvement of Dalits with such filth accords with their low-status position at the bottom of the Hindu caste hierarchy, even as their services allow high-status people, such as Brahmans, to maintain their ritual purity.

However, castes associated with ruling and warfare – and the killing and deaths of human beings – are typically accorded high rank on the caste hierarchy. In these instances, political power and wealth outrank association with violence as the key determinant of caste rank.

Ideology as an instrument of domination, of ensuring that the common people think and behave as the ruling elite want them to, finds an archetypical expression in Brahmanism. Brahmanism stands for the aggregate of the sacerdotal literature, social structure, and religio-political institutions that has been masterminded by the elite with the primary aim of keeping the masses ignorant, servile, and disunited. Brahmanism uses the ideology of caste as a crucial instrument to dehumanize, divide, and dominate the productive majority. Different caste groups are separated from each other in matters of marriage, physical contact, and food by rules of purity and pollution. Hierarchy, along with purity and power, culminates in the Brahman. Power politics thus is at the heart of Brahmanism. The exercise of power necessarily involves conflict and resistance. The contestation for economic, cultural, and intellectual resources between the powerful and the powerless involves both dominance and resistance.

The Strangers Face

When two Indians meet as strangers, "the encounter is often a duel, everything – response, behavior, body language, social niceties, form of address, receptivity – depends on an assessment of where the person stands on the scale of power and influence."[4] For an Indian, superior and subordinate relationships "have the character of eternal verity and moral imperative – (and the) automatic reverence for superiors is a nearly universal psycho-social fact."[5] The entire worth of a person is dependent on the position he occupies on a hierarchical scale. In Hinduism, identity is dependent upon worth, and worth is determined as people are born and reborn in accordance with their *karmas*, the quality of their deeds. This certainly affects human relationships.

Resistance to Caste

Despite resistance to caste and Brahmanism, beginning with shramanic heterodoxies and Buddhism, followed by various streams of Bhakti movements, Sikhism, Sufism, similar lesser known campaigns and ideologies

---

[4]   Pavan K. Varma, *Being Indian,* Viking Penguin Books India, 2004.

[5]   Sudhir Kakar, *The Indian Psyche: The Inner World; Shamans, Mystics and Doctors; Tales of Love, Sex and Danger*, New Delhi: Oxford University Press, 1996, p.138.

and anti-caste egalitarian movements in modern India, caste consciousness and Brahamanic mindset persist in their modernized, metamorphosed avatar, defying and denying democratic ideals.

The Bhakti movement that emerged in the fourteenth and fifteenth centuries, exemplified in the cults of popular "saints" such as Kabir and Mirabai, tried to negate the power of the Brahmin clergy and questioned the Brahmin's chief weapon: purity and the power to dispense untouchability.

It's all one skin and bone, one piss and shit, one blood, one meat.
From one drop, a universe. Who's a Brahmin? Who's shudra?

So sang Kabir, the fifteenth-century Bhakti saint (Hess, 1983: 25). Yet the Bhakti movements were unable to change the workings of the caste system, primarily because these saints formed a sort of mystic fringe, spiritually intense alternatives to the main body of orthodoxy that, although popular and doctrinally seductive, were no threat to a 3,000-year-old institutionalised discrimination.

In the nineteenth century, social reform emanated from the educated upper-caste elites who came into contact with Western ideas of liberalism and rationality (Raychaudhuri, 1999: 60). There were campaigns to secure the rights of the widow, to ban sati (the practice of widows immolating themselves on their husband's funeral pyres), and to reject caste.

The emergence of Gandhi and Ambedkar – mutually opposed to each other, yet highly significant, each in his own way, to the cause of the Dalits – grew from the context created by these nineteenth-century movements as well as the deeper traditions of anticaste protests created by Buddhism, Jainism, and the Bhakti cults. The movement to abolish caste prejudices owes its modern liberal humanist form to Jotirao Govindrao Phule in Maharashtra and later to the campaigns of E. V. Ramaswami Naicker in Madras state.

Jotirao Phule (1827-1890) developed powerful arguments against the caste system and the Brahman and also used Christian missionary arguments to "reject the fictitious world of Hindu religion" (O'Hanlon, 1985: 105). His Satyashodhak Samaj or "Truth-Seeking Society" gave voice in 1873 to the radical idea that Brahmins had used religious authority and administrative power acquired under colonial rule to oppress other sections of society. Although "moderate" and "respectable" reformers were reluctant to accept such wholesale condemnation of Brahmins (O'Hanlon, 1985: 255) and the Satyashodhak Samaj remained virtually limited to the state of Maharashtra, the influence of its ideas can be traced to the anticaste ideologies that emerged subsequently.

The work of Christian missionaries also functioned as a fundamental challenge to traditional caste-based practices. From O'Hanlon's thesis on the radicalizing influence of Christianity on Phule's thoughts, it would be accurate to say that caste, as a conceptual category, was seriously challenged only after the arrival of Christian missionaries, who initiated the radical idea of extending education to the Dalits. The first special schools for Dalits were opened in the 1840s, encouraged not only by the missionaries but also by the British administration. From these schools came the first generation of Dalit activists, writers, and politicians. A Dalit writer recently wrote that as far as the Dalits are concerned, "the British arrived too late and left too early," a reference to the fact that had it not been for the British colonial administration, Dalits would never have gained the right to attend school.[6]

Even though the overwhelming majority of Dalits in the colonial period remained railway workers, landless migrant labourers, urban sweepers, stone cutters, and servants, some became soldiers in the army of the East India Company, and others, such as the *Mahars*, were able to achieve the status of wealthy and assertive elite[7]

After Phule, the other social reformer who can be seen as a precursor of Ambedkar was E. V. Ramaswami Naicker (1879-1973). Naicker founded the Self-Respect Movement, which advocated a vigorous attack on caste, especially "Aryan Brahmins." He campaigned for forcible temple entry, burning of the Manusmriti, and atheism. Ironically, modern-day political parties such as the Dravida Munnetra Kazhagam and the All India Anna Dravida Munnetra Kazhagam, which are the descendants of the Self-Respect Movement, have veered away from the rationalism and atheism of Naicker and instead have lapsed into various forms of Hindu obscurantism.[8] Both Phule and Naicker, however, positioned themselves as not just anti-Brahmin but as implacably anticaste and pro-poor.

---

[6]   Prasad, Chandrabhan. "Blacks in US Media and Blackouts in India." *The Pioneer*, 11 November 2000.

[7]   Zelliot, Eleanor. *Learning the Use of Political Means: The Mahars of Maharashtra. Caste in Indian Politics*. ed. Rajni Kothari. New Delhi: Orient Longman, 1970, p.43.

[8]   The Dravida Munnetra Kazhagam and the All India Anna Dravida Munnetra Kazhagam, political parties that rule the state of Tamil Nadu, were born from Naicker's Self-Respect Movement. Today they openly ally with religious groups and have created a ritualized hero-worshipping political culture by which political leaders are viewed as gods and indulge in a range of superstitious practices.

Intolerant Society

Although Indian society advocates toleration while maintaining an otherwise intolerant cruel society, who can leave the caste hierarchy and claim the benefits of toleration? Who can vertically challenge and aspire for the higher caste in the hierarchy and expect accommodation? The characteristics of "accommodation" to be found in a holistically conceived hierarchical society are not the same as those which will bring about a liberal egalitarian society.[9]

Religious intolerance is not alien to Hinduism. Romila Thapar notes "the nineteenth-century myth that the Hindus are by instinct and religion a non-violent people" and comments, "The genesis of this myth was partly in the romantic image of the Indian past projected, for example, by scholars such as Max Muller."[10] In Hindu tradition, for instance, the mythical battles in Mahabharata and Ramayana epics are frequently used as metaphors for present-day struggles. Writing about "The Mahabharata Legacy, and the Gita's Intent," Rajmohan Gandhi says, "Proud as we are of the epic's codes of chivalry, we cannot be proud, I suggest in all humility, of the story, or history, it reveals. In particular, we cannot be proud of the epic's acquiescence in triumph of revenge over reconciliation. I suggest, further, that we cannot be glad that the epic is reproduced in varied forms in our history"[11]

Vengal Chakkarai, a high-caste Hindu convert to Christ, advocated that the church should "confront Hinduism on the plains of life." By this he meant confronting the caste oppression and exploitation. The household of Jesus Christ is duty-bound to spread social equality; the practice of caste divisions in the church runs counter to the teachings of Jesus Christ whose apostle said, "There is neither Jew nor Greek, slave nor free, male nor female, for you are all one in Christ" (Galatians 3: 28). Chakkarai believed that as a result of education in Christian institutions, people gained some understanding of Christianity, but very few made any overt move to Christianity. He wrote in 1913 "that as a matter of historical record, most educated Hindus who had become dissatisfied with their ancestral faith had

---

[9]   See Marc Galanter, *Law and Society in Modern India*, Oxford University Press, Delhi, 1997.

[10]   Romila Thapar, Ibid. Also see Romila Thapar, *Cultural Transaction and Early India*, 19ff. See M. Muller, *India: What Can It Teach Us*? London, 1983, pp. 101ff.

[11]   Rajmohan Gandhi, *Revenge and Reconciliation*, Penguin Books, 1999, p.34.

been diverted to the neo-Hindu religious movements or theosophy rather than Christianity."[12] He, as we saw earlier, advocated the critique of life, when he stated that it is upon "the plain of life and its struggles that Christianity must confront Hinduism."[13] This could be discerned in the area of social concern, particularly in such matters as caste distinction, dowry, and the needs of the poor. The social reform movements within Hinduism may have been promoted by Christian teachings either by way of reaction or inspiration[14]. Gopal Hari Deshmukh attacked many aspects of traditional Indian life – the caste system, child marriage, and the treatment of widows were particular targets.[15] But in his personal life he did not break with traditional ways.

M. M. Thomas writes: "Considering the fact that the Christian Mission was the first in many parts of India to treat the untouchables as human beings and to bring them the gospel of their dignity in Christ, as well as education, Christianity has played a part in arousing and strengthening Anti-Brahmanism. And this in turn awoke the Brahmin and other caste Hindu leadership to the need of putting the Hindu household itself in order by social and religious reform ... fear of Christianity has been the beginning of social wisdom for Hinduism."[16]

Democracy and Caste

How could democracy, brought in by British rule, flourish in a highly hierarchical Hindu society, promoting the ideal of egalitarian society? This appears to be an enigma. The Indian response to this democratic ideal of an equal society must therefore be seen in the specific and unique context of its own culture and tradition.

Pavan K. Varma argues in his book that "democracy has survived in India not because Indians are democratic, but because democracy has proved

---

[12]   Chakkarai in the "Sixteenth Report of the Cambridge Mission to Delhi, 1894" [CMD 131], quoted in Ingelby, *Missionaries, Education and India,* p. 281.

[13]   Chakkarai, "The Objection of Educated Hindus to Christianity," *Young Men of India,* p.540.

[14]   M.M Thomas discusses this in detail in his book *The Acknowledged Christ of Indian Renaissance* (Madras, 1976).

[15]   See, e.g., Charles, *Indian Nationalism and Social Reform* (Princeton, N.J., 1964) p. 102.

[16]   M. M. Thomas, *The Secular Ideologies of India and the Secular Meaning of the Gospel* (Madras, Christian Literature Society, 1976) p. 152.

to be the most effective instrument for cherished pursuit of power." 17 In fact, Varma builds a case that the Hindu society "exalts the pursuit of material well-being, Aretha, as a principal goal of life." A significant thought that he sums up is, "Indians are extraordinarily sensitive to the calculus of power. They consider the pursuit of power a legitimate end in itself and display great astuteness in adjusting to, and discovering, the focus of power. Those who renounce the lure of power are worshipped, not because their example is capable of emulation, but in sheer awe of their ability to transcend the irresistible." 18

Answering the question why Gandhism failed in India, Varma states, "Mahatma Gandhi believed that the means are as important as the end. His creed failed to attract followers because the concept was alien to Indian tradition. India's most well-known treatise on statecraft, the Arthashastra, written by Kautilya almost two thousand years ago, wastes little time on moral underpinnings of power. On the contrary, it advocates a compelling unsentimental recipe on how to seize power through means fair and foul. Kautilya's essential thesis is that expediency is far more important than conventional morality in conducting the affairs of the state.'"[19]

Democracy has flourished in India because most Indians have perceived it to be a pragmatic and effective means to personal power by participating in the democratic process.[20] In the past, status was prescriptive, a consequence of one's birth. Today it can be acquired by other means, including greater avenues of upward mobility. But this has not made people more egalitarian in their outlook. In a country where resources are scarce and opportunities for upward mobility are limited, political power opens the gates to both.[21]

The hierarchical frame of mind of the Hindu society has not been replaced by a new egalitarianism; rather, democracy provides legitimacy to hierarchies, both old and new. Varma argues that "democracy did not adopt India. Indians usurped democracy because it could be moulded to fit earlier structures without threatening them. The miracle of India is that the practice of democracy has flourished within its boundaries for over five decades in the absence of a democratic temperament."[22]

---

[17] Pavan K Varma, *Being Indian*, (Viking Penguin Books India, 2004), p.55.

[18] Ibid., p.7.

[19] Ibid., p.26.

[20] Ibid., p.20.

[21] Ibid., p.22.

[22] Ibid., p.23.

Democracy has led to gradual but genuine political empowerment of the weakest and poorest sections. Socially the lower castes have continued to rise through the ballot box and the growing literacy. Local self-government in the form of Panchayati Raj has slowly become a reality, thanks to the Seventy-Third Amendment to the constitution in 1993.

Caste Divisions in Church

Caste thinking is in some of our churches. Many scholars have documented it. Anantha Krishna Iyer, outlining the caste-oriented manners and customs of Syrian Christians, writes, "Each division among the Syrian Christians has become, as in Hindu caste, an endogamous sect, with no intermarriage between the members of one sect and those of another, though no objection is made to inter-dining." 23 It is not uncommon that high-caste Christians demand separation, for fear of pollution, from the Christians of Dalit origin.

The Christians of Dalit origin speak of triple discrimination of which they are victims. First, they are denied their government-instituted reservation privileges when they publicly declare their allegiance to Jesus Christ. Second, they encounter discrimination in the Church. Third, the high caste uses the Dalits to persecute the Dalits who turn to Christ. Dumont himself recognized the existence of caste among non–Hindus as due to "the proximity of the Hindu environment, which predominates both generally and regionally."[24]

Conversion to Christianity still disqualifies poor and underprivileged converts from Dalit benefits.[25] Religion should not become a disqualifica-

---

[23]   A. K. Iyer, *Anthropology of Syrian Christians*, 1926, p.218. Cf. Louis Dumont in his classic Homo Hierarchius, (Eng Translation) 1970, points out, "even Catholics of more recent origin are divided into four distinct groups or castes. Christians originating from untouchables seem to have their own churches."

[24]   Ibid, p. 210.

[25]   "Schedule Caste" has been defined as follows in Article 366: "Schedule Castes" means such castes, races or tribes or parts of or groups within such castes, races or tribes as are deemed under Article 341 to be Scheduled castes for the purpose of this constitution." Under Article 341, power has been granted to the President and the Parliament to include or exclude the names of the castes from the list of Scheduled castes in the Scheduled Castes Order 1950. Article 341 reads as follows: "341(1) President may with respect to any state or Union Territory and where it is a State after consultation with the Governor therefore, by Public notification specify the castes, races or tribes or parts of or groups within castes, races or tribes which shall for the purposes of this constitution be deemed to be Scheduled castes in relation to the State or Union Territory as the case may be. (2) Parliament may by law include in or exclude from the list of Scheduled Castes speci-

tion. Social and economic conditions should determine the granting of privileges. The Dalit Christians have long demanded reservation benefits from successive governments in power at New Delhi, but in vain. The demand is called controversial, and fears are expressed that if Dalit Christians are given reservation benefits, non-Christian Dalits will leave the caste hierarchy of Hinduism and convert to Christianity.

Survival of Caste

This question has been debated several times over for a century and a half. Various voices address this question. Harold Gould writes, "It ... appears very unlikely that so admirable an adaptive structure as caste is in any serious danger of ever disappearing completely."[26] N. Jayaram holds this opinion: "Its religious basis may wane, its systemic rigor may weaken; but its social (kinship) basis will persist, and its group connotation will gain strength. As far as its interface with Hinduism is concerned, though Hinduism may lose meaning as a justificatory ideology for the hierarchy and inequalities of the system, its cultural crux will persist and crystallize. And, Hinduism will benefit more from the survival of caste than caste from Hinduism."[27]

However the Dalits have a different approach to caste system, which is succinctly summarized by Bhagwan Das, who challenges the dehumanizing caste identity as he writes: "Upper caste Hindus has a vested interest in maintaining and perpetuating caste. If caste goes, Hinduism will die. With the Dalits it is just the opposite. Caste is the greatest obstacle in the way of their unity and progress. If they do not destroy caste, caste will destroy them. The Hindus have no real sympathy with them. They need them only to do dirty work and to render them friendless by pitting them against the Muslims one day, against Sikhs the next day and maybe against the Christians very soon." He proposes that "in the eradication of caste and adoption of the right code of conduct based on equality, compassion, loving kindness, and justice lies their salvation."[28] The laudable list of transforma-

---

fied in a notification issued under Clause (1) any caste, race or tribe or part of or group within any caste, race or tribe but save as aforesaid notification issued under the said clause shall not be varied by any subsequent notification."

[26] Harold A. Gould, *Caste Adaptation in Modernizing Indian Society.* Delhi: Chanakya Publications. 1988, p. 167.

[27] N. Jayaram, "Caste and Hinduism: Changing Protean Relationship" in M. N. Srinivas ed. *Caste: Its Twentieth-Century Avatar*, Penguin Books, 1996, p. 84.

[28] Bhagwan Das, "Dalits and Caste System," in, James Massey, edited by *Indigenous People: Dalits,* ISPCK, Delhi, 1994, p.75.

tional values that Bhagwan Das has proposed, and that he has observed, are not part of Hindu culture.

Economic projects as such do not help poor people develop the crucial sense of self-worth. Rather, the development of self-worth is the foundation for every other human growth. This makes the gospel so vital for change. The gospel transforms the perception of the poor from worthless failures to an appreciation that in Christ they have the same worth as other people. V. T. Rajshekar, a non-Christian leader of Dalits, suggests for the Dalits, "Poverty is not the number one problem. People cannot live by bread alone. They want the self-respect which is denied under Hinduism. They will get it the moment they get out of Hinduism and convert to other religions."[29]

Bishop Vedanayagam Samuel Azariah (1874-1945)[30], born into a Nadar Christian family, was a successful leader of grassroots movements of religious transformation in South India in the early twentieth century. Nadars occupied a middle position of "semi-untouchables" in the caste system between "Dalits" [31] and "Sudras." Like Dalits, they were barred from entering temples or courts of justice, and dress regulations forbade women from covering the upper parts of their bodies. They were forbidden the use of public wells and were required to stay 36 paces away from high-caste Brahmins. Their houses were limited to one storey. They were forbidden to carry umbrellas, to wear shoes or gold ornaments, or to milk cows, and

---

[29] V.T. Rajshekar in *The Gospel among Our Hindu Neighbors,* edited by Vinay Samuel and Chris Sugden Bangalore, 1982 pp. 131-132.

[30] At baptism he was given the new name "Thomas Vedanayagam," which combined the surname of Welsh missionary John Thomas (1807-70) and Veda, meaning Bible, and nayagam, meaning "master" or "leader." Cf. Susan Billington Harper, *In the Shadow of the Mahatma, Bishop V.S. Azariah and the Travails of Christianity in British India* (Curzon Press Ltd, Richmond, Surrey, U.K. 2000) has meticulously researched the major events and the issues of Azariah's public life, and her work is indeed a primary source to understand the role of religion in modern Indian social and political life (hereafter as ISM).

[31] The currently acceptable term "Dalit" is used in this article. Dalit is a self-designation by those groups who belong to the Panchama (or fifth) Varna outside the Hindu caste system. Some names, such as "Untouchables," Depressed Class, Schedule caste, Harijan, were invented by government or political leaders on behalf of the "untouchable" groups. Different names were usually devised to reduce the stigma associated with older designations or to unite several oppressed groups into one definable category for government benefits. Each term therefore carries potent political and historical connotations. See James Massey (ed.), *Indigenous People: Dalits* (ISPCK, Delhi 1994).

women were not allowed to carry pots on their hips. Unlike Dalits, many Nadars abstained from liquor and beef and disapproved of the remarriage of widows.

The Christian Church helped Nadar women gain the right to cover their upper bodies during the violent breast-cloth controversy of the early-to mid-nineteenth century. Nadar women were frequently attacked, stripped, and beaten, and chapels and schools were burned for the offence of wearing the breast cloths previously worn only by higher-caste Nair women. Empowered by the gospel teaching, Nadars became leaders in the movement for social change.[32]

---

[32] D. Forrester, "The Depressed Classes and Conversion to Christianity, 1860-1960," in *Religion in South Asia: Religious Conversion and Revival Movements in South Asia in Medieval and Modern Times,* ed. G.A. Oddie (New Delhi, 1977) pp.33-66.

About the Author

Biography

Prof. Dr. theol. Dr. phil. Thomas Schirrmacher, PhD, DD, (born 1960) is speaker for human rights of the World Evangelical Alliance, speaking for appr. 600 million Christians, chair of its theological commission, and director of its new International Institute for Religious Freedom (Bonn, Cape Town, Colombo). He is also director of the Commission for Religious Freedom of the German and Austrian Evangelical Alliance. He is member of the board of the International Society for Human Rights.

Schirrmacher is professor of the sociology of religion at the State University of the West in Timisoara (Romania) and Distinguished Professor of Global Ethics and International Development at William Carey University in Shillong (Meghalaya, India). He is also president of 'Martin Bucer European Theological Seminary and Research Institutes' with small campuses in Bonn, Berlin, Zurich, Innsbruck, Prague and Istanbul, where he teaches ethics and comparative religions.

He studied theology from 1978 to 1982 at STH Basel (Switzerland) and since 1983 Cultural Anthropology and Comparative Religions at Bonn State University. He earned a Drs. theol. in Missiology and Ecumenics at Theological University (Kampen/Netherlands) in 1984, and a Dr. theol. in Missiology and Ecumenics at Johannes Calvin Foundation (Kampen/ Netherlands) in 1985, a Ph.D. in Cultural Anthropology at Pacific Western University in Los Angeles (CA) in 1989, a Th.D. in Ethics at Whitefield Theological Seminary in Lakeland (FL) in 1996, and a Dr. phil. in Comparative Religions / Sociology of Religion at State University of Bonn in 2007. In 1997 he received an honorary doctorate (D.D.) from Cranmer Theological House, in 2006 one from Acts University in Bangalore.

His newest books in German are on fundamentalism (2010), racism (2009), persecution of Christians in Iraq (2009), HIV/AIDS as Christian challenge (2008), internet pornography (2008), Hitler's religion of war (2007), and multiculturalism (2007). His 92 books were published in 17 languages.

He is listed in Marquis' Who's Who in the World, Dictionary of International Biography, International Who is Who of Professionals, 2000 Outstanding Intellectuals of the 21st Century and many other biographical yearbooks.

Books by Thomas Schirrmacher in chronological order (With short commentaries)

As author:

Das Mißverständnis des Emil Brunner: Emil Brunners Bibliologie als Ursache für das Scheitern seiner Ekklesiologie. Theologische Untersuchungen zu Weltmission und Gemeindebau. ed. by Hans-Georg Wünch and Thomas Schirrmacher. Arbeitsgemeinschaft für Weltmission und Gemeindebau: Lörrach, 1982. 54 pp.
[The misunderstanding of Emil Brunner] *A study and critique of Emil Brunner's ecclesiology and of the bibliology and hermeneutics of dialectical theology.*

Mohammed: Prophet aus der Wüste. Schwengeler: Berneck (CH), 1984[1], 1986[2], 1990[3], 1996[4]. VTR: Nürnberg, 2006[5]. 120 pp.
[Muhammad] *A short biography of the founder of Islam and an introduction into Islam.*

Theodor Christlieb und seine Missionstheologie. Verlag der Evangelischen Gesellschaft für Deutschland: Wuppertal, 1985. 308 pp.
[Theodor Christlieb and his theology of mission] *A study of the biography, theology and missiology of the leading German Pietist, professor of practical theology and international missions leader in the second half of the nineteenth century. (Thesis for Dr. theol. in missiology.)*

Marxismus: Opium für das Volk? Schwengeler: Berneck (CH), 1990[1], 1997[2]. 150 pp.
[Marxism: Opiate for the People?] *Marxism is proven to be a religion and an opiate for the masses. Emphasizes the differences between Marxist and Biblical work ethics.*

Zur marxistischen Sagen- und Märchenforschung und andere volkskundliche Beiträge. Verlag für Kultur und Wissenschaft: Bonn, 1991[1], 2003[2]. 227 pp.
[On the Marxist View of Sagas and Tales and other essays in folklore and cultural anthropology] *10 essays and articles on the science of folklore and cultural anthropology in Germany. Includes a critique of the Marxist interpretation of tales and sagas, and studies on the history of marriage and family in Europe from the 6th century onward.*

„Der göttliche Volkstumsbegriff" und der „Glaube an Deutschlands Größe und heilige Sendung": Hans Naumann als Volkskundler und Germanist unter dem Nationalsozialismus. 2 volumes. Verlag für Kultur und Wissenschaft: Bonn, 2 volumes, 1992[1], in one volume 2000[2]. 606 pp.
[Hans Naumann as Anthropologist and Germanist under National Socialism] *Discusses the history of German cultural anthropology and folklore under Hitler, especially the leading figure Naumann, professor of German language, whose scientific theory is shown to be very religious in tone. (Thesis for a PhD in Cultural Anthropology.)*

War Paulus wirklich auf Malta? Hänssler: Neuhausen, 1992, VTR: Nürnberg, 2000[2] (together with Heinz Warnecke). 254 pp.
[Was Paul Really on Malta?] *The book shows that Paul was not shipwrecked on Malta but on another island, Kephalenia, and that the report in Acts is very accurate. The Pauline authorship of the Pastoral Epistles is defended with theological and linguistic arguments against higher criticism.*

Psychotherapie – der fatale Irrtum. Schwengeler: Berneck (CH), 1993[1], 1994[2]; 1997[3]; 2001[4] (together with Rudolf Antholzer). 150 pp.
[Psychotherapy – the Fatal Mistake] *A critique of secular psychotherapy, showing that psychotherapy often is a religion, and that most psychotherapists call every school except their own unscientific.*

Paulus im Kampf gegen den Schleier: Eine alternative Sicht von 1. Korinther 11,2-16. Biblia et symbiotica 4. Verlag für Kultur und Wissenschaft: Bonn, 1993[1], 1994[2], 1995[3], 1997[4] 168 pp. Revised: VTR: Nürnberg, 2002[5]
[Paul in Conflict with the Veil!?] *Exegetical examination of 1. Corinthians 11,2-16, following an alternative view of John Lightfoot, member of the Westminster assembly in the 16th century.*
„Schirrmacher argues that from the biblical teaching that man is the head of woman (1 Cor 11:3) the Corinthians had drawn the false conclusions that in prayer a woman must be veiled (11:4-6) and a man is forbidden to be veiled (11:7), and that the wife exists for the husband but not the husband for the wife (11:8-9). Paul, however, rejected these conclu-

sions and showed in 11:10-16 why the veiling of women did not belong to God's commandments binding upon all the Christian communities. After stating the thesis and presenting his alternative translation and exposition of 1 Cor 11:2-16, he considers the difficulties in the text, presents his alternative exposition in detail (in the form of thirteen theses), discusses quotations and irony in 1 Corinthians, and deals with other NT texts about women's clothing and prayer and about the subordination of wives." (New Testament Abstracts vol. 39 (1995) 1, p. 154).

Der Römerbrief. 2 vol. Neuhausen: Hänssler, 1994[1]; Hamburg: RVB & Nürnberg: VTR, 2001[2]. 331 + 323 pp.
[The Letter to the Romans] *Commentary on Romans in form of major topics of Systematic Theology starting from the text of Romans, but then going on to the whole Bible.*

Der Text des Römerbriefes: Für das Selbststudium gegliedert. Biblia et symbiotica 7. Verlag für Kultur und Wissenschaft: Bonn, 1994. 68 pp.
[The Text of the Letters to the Romans] *The text of Romans newly translated and structured for self study.*

Ethik. Neuhausen: Hänssler, 1994[1]. 2 vol. 883 & 889 pp.; Hamburg: RVB & Nürnberg: VTR, 2001[2]. 3 vol. 2150 pp.; 2002[3]. 2009[4], 2011[5]. 8 volumes. 2850 pp.
[Ethics] *Major Evangelical ethics in German covering all aspects of general, special, personal and public ethics.*

Galilei-Legenden und andere Beiträge zu Schöpfungsforschung, Evolutionskritik und Chronologie der Kulturgeschichte 1979-1994. Biblia et symbiotica 12. Verlag für Kultur und Wissenschaft: Bonn, 1996. 331 pp.
[Legends of Galileo and other Contributions to Creation Science, Criticism of Evolution and Chronology of the History of Culture 1979-1994].

Völker – Drogen – Kannibalismus: Ethnologische und länderkundliche Beiträge 1984 – 1994. Verlag für Kultur und Wissenschaft: Bonn, 1997. 218 pp.
[Peoples – Drugs – Cannibalism] *A collection of articles on cultural anthropology, especially on Indians in South America, cannibalism and the religious use of drugs.*

Die Vielfalt biblischer Sprache: Über 100 alt- und neutestamentliche Stilarten, Ausdrucksweisen, Redeweisen und Gliederungsformen. Verlag für Kultur und Wissenschaft: Bonn, 1997. 130 pp.

[The Diversity of Biblical Language] *A hermeneutical study, listing more than 100 specific language techniques in the Bible with several proof texts for each of them.*

Gottesdienst ist mehr: Plädoyer für einen liturgischen Gottesdienst. Verlag für Kultur und Wissenschaft: Bonn, 1998. 130 pp.
[Church Service is More] *An investigation into biblical proof texts for liturgical elements in Christian Sunday service.*

Gesetz und Geist: Eine alternative Sicht des Galaterbriefes. Reformatorische Paperbacks. Reformatorischer Verlag: Hamburg, 1999. 160 pp.
[Law and Spirit] *This commentary emphasizing the ethical aspects of Galatians wants to prove that Galatians is not only fighting legalists but also a second party of Paul's opponents, who were totally opposed to the Old Testament and the Law, and lived immorally in the name of Christian freedom, a view especially endorsed by Wilhelm Lütgert's commentary of 1919. Paul is fighting against the abrogation of the Old Testament Law as well as against using this Law as way of salvation instead of God's grace.*

Law and Spirit: An Alternative View of Galatians. RVB International: Hamburg, 2001. 160 pp.
English version of the same book.

God Wants You to Learn, Labour and Love. Reformation Books: Hamburg, 1999. 120 pp.
Four essays for Third World Christian Leaders on Learning with Jesus, Work Ethic, Love and Law and Social Involvement.

Dios Quiere que Tú Aprendas Trabajes y Ames. Funad: Managua (Nikaragua), 1999[1]; 2000[2]; RVB International: Hamburg, 2003[3]. 70 pp.
[God Wants You to Learn, Labour and Love] *Spanish version of the same book.*

37 Gründe, warum Christen sich für eine Erneuerung unserer Gesellschaft auf christlicher Grundlage einsetzen sollten. Die Wende, 1999. 40 pp.
[37 reasons for Christian involvement in society and politics].

Christenverfolgung geht uns alle an: Auf dem Weg zu einer Theologie des Martyriums. Idea-Dokumentation 15/99. Idea: Wetzlar, 1999. 64 pp.
[The Persecution of Christians Concerns Us All: Towards a Theology of Martyrdom] *70 theses on persecution and martyrdom, written*

for the International Day of Prayer for the Persecuted Church on behalf of the German and European Evangelical Alliance

World Mission – Heart of Christianity. RVB International: Hamburg, 1999. 120 pp.
Articles on the Biblical and systematic fundament of World Mission, especially on mission as rooted in God's being, on 'Mission in the OT', and 'Romans as a Charter for World Mission'. Shorter version of German original 2001.

Eugen Drewermann und der Buddhismus. Verlag für Theologie und Religionswissenschaft: Nürnberg, 2000[1]; 2001[2]. 132 pp.
[Drewermann and Buddhism] Deals with the German Catholic Author Drewermann and his propagating Buddhist thinking. Includes chapter on a Christian Ethics of Environment.

Ausverkaufte Würde? Der Pornographie-Boom und seine psychischen Folgen. Hänssler: Holzgerlingen, 2000. (with Christa Meves). 130 pp.
[The Selling Off of Dignity] The psychological results of pornography.

Eine Sekte wird evangelisch – Die Reformation der Weltweiten Kirche Gottes. Idea-Dokumentation 11/2000. Idea: Wetzlar, 2000. 56 pp.
[A Cult Becomes Protestant] Detailed report on the reformation of the Worldwide Church of God (Herbert W. Armstrong) from a sect to an evangelical church.

Legends About the Galilei-Affair. RVB International: Hamburg, 2001. 120 pp.
Shorter version of the German book 'Galilei-Legenden' mentioned above with essays on the Galilei-affair and creation science.

Human Rights Threatened in Europe: Euthanasia – Abortion – Bioethicconvention. RVB International: Hamburg, 2001. 100 pp.
Updated Lectures on euthanasia and biomedicine at the 1st European Right to Life Forum Berlin, 1998, and articles on abortion.

Menschenrechte in Europa in Gefahr. RVB: Hamburg, 2001... 110 pp.
[Human Rights Threatened in Europe] Updated Lectures on euthanasia and biomedicine at the 1st European Right to Life Forum Berlin, 1998, and articles on abortion. See slightly different English version above.

Aufbruch zur modernen Weltmission: William Careys Theologie. RVB. 64 pp.
[Be Keen to Get Going: William Careys Theology] First discussion of Carey's theology in

length, explaining his Calvinistic and Postmillennial background.

Be Keen to Get Going: William Careys Theology. RVB: Hamburg, 2001. 64 pp.
Same book in English.

Darf ein Christ schwören? RVB: Hamburg, 2001. 140 pp.
[May Christians Take an Oath?] On Swearing and on its meaning for covenant theology . Taken from 'Ethik', vol. 1.

Christus im Alten Testament. RVB: Hamburg, 2001. 84 pp.
[Christ in the Old Testament] On Christ and the Trinity in the Old Testament and on 'the Angel of the Lord'. Taken from 'Ethik'.

Wie erkenne ich den Willen Gottes? Führungsmystik auf dem Prüfstand. RVB: Hamburg, 2001. 184 pp.
[How to know the will of God] – Criticizes the inner leading of the Spirit. Taken from 'Ethik'.

Love is the Fulfillment of Love – Essays in Ethics. RVB: Hamburg, 2001. 140 pp.
Essays on ethical topics, including role of the Law, work ethics, and European Union.

Mission und der Kampf um die Menschenrechte. RVB: Hamburg, 2001. 108 S.
[Mission and the Battle for Human Rights] The relationship of world missions and the fight for human rights is discussed on an ethical level (theology of human rights) as well as on a practical level.

The Persecution of Christians Concerns Us All: Towards a Theology of Martyrdom. zugleich Idea-Dokumentation 15/99 E. VKW: Bonn, 2001. 156 pp.
70 theses on persecution and martyrdom, written for the International Day of Prayer for the Persecuted Church on behalf of the German and European Evangelical Alliance

Irrtumslosigkeit der Schrift oder Hermeneutik der Demut? VTR: Nürnberg, 2001. 82 pp.
[Inerrancy of Scripture or 'Hermeneutics of Humility'] Debate with Dr. Hempelmann on the inerrancy of scripture.

Beiträge zur Kirchen- und Theologiegeschichte: Heiligenverehrung – Universität Gießen – Reformation / Augustin – Böhl – Spurgeon – Brunner. VKW: Bonn, 2001. 200 pp.
[Essay on the History of church and Dogma] Articles on topics from church history like 'The beginning of the veneration of saints' and on the named theologians.

Weltmission — Das Herz des christlichen Glaubens: Beiträge aus 'Evangelikale

Missiologie'. VKW: Bonn, 2001. 200 pp.
[World Mission – Heart of Christianity] *Articles on the Biblical and systematic Foundation of World Mission, especially on mission as rooted in God's being, on 'Mission in the OT', and 'Romans as a Charter for World Mission'. Shorter version of German original 2001.*

Säkulare Religionen: Aufsätze zum religiösen Charakter von Nationalsozialismus und Kommunismus. VKW: Bonn, 2001. 140 pp.
[Secular Religions] *Articles on the religious nature of National Socialism and Communism. Includes texts of prayers to Hitler.*

Paulus im Kampf gegen den Schleier!? VTR: Nürnberg, 2002[5]. 130 pp.
Revised version. See commentary on first edition 1993[1].

Paul in Conflict with the Veil!? VTR: Nürnberg, 2002[1]; 2007[2]. 130 pp.
Same book in English.

Hoffnung für Europa: 66 Thesen. VTR: Nürnberg, 2002. *Official thesis and study of hope in the Old and New Testament for Hope for Europe of the European Ev. Alliance and Lausanne Europe.*

Hope for Europe: 66 Theses. VTR: Nürnberg, 2002. *Same book in English. Also available in Czech, Dutch, Spanish, Romanian, Portuguese, French, Russian, Italian, Hungarian, Lithuanian, and Latvian.*

ABC der Demut. RVB: Hamburg, 2002
[ABC of Humility] *Notes and bible studies on humility in alphabetical order.*

Führen in ethischer Verantwortung: Die drei Seiten jeder Verantwortung. Edition ACF. Brunnen: Gießen, 2002
[Leading in ethical responsibility] *An introduction into ethics for economic and other leaders for the Academy of Christian Leaders.*

Der Papst und das Leiden: Warum der Papst nicht zurücktritt. VTR: Nürnberg, 2002. 64 pp.
[The Pope and Suffering] *A study of the writings of Pope John II. on suffering and an evaluation of their exegetical basis. Gives reasons why the pope does not resign.*

Erziehung, Bildung, Schule. VTR: Nürnberg, 2002. 88 pp.
[Instruction, Education, School] *The chapters on raising of children, example, education, and Christian school from 'Ethics'.*

Thomas Schirrmacher, Christine Schirrmacher u. a. Harenberg Lexikon der Religionen. Harenberg Verlag: Düsseldorf, 2002. 1020 pp.

[Harenberg Dictionary of World Religions] *In a major secular dictionary on world religions, Thomas Schirrmacher wrote the section on Christianity ('Lexicon of Christianity', pp. 8-267) and Christine Schirrmacher the section on Islam ('Lexicon of Islam', 'pp. 428-549).*

Studies in Church Leadership: New Testament Church Structure – Paul and His Co-workers – An Alternative Theological Education – A Critique of Catholic Canon Law. VKW: Bonn, 2003. 112 pp.
Contains the named five essays. The first essay is translated from vol. 5 of 'Ethics'.

Im Gespräch mit dem Wanderprediger des New Age – und andere apologetische Beiträge. VKW: Bonn, 2003. 210 pp.
[In Discussion with the Itinerant Preacher of the New Age] *Essays and reports on non-Christian religions, New Age, reincarnation, manicheism from two decades of apologetic debates.*

Verborgene Zahlenwerte in der Bibel? – und andere Beiträge zur Bibel. VKW: Bonn, 2003. 200 pp.
[Secret Numbers in the Bible?] *Essays and articles on Bible Numeric's, the importance of Hebrew studies, Obadiah, the Psalms and other Bible related topics from 2 decades of studies.*

Feindbild Islam. VKW: Bonn, 2003. 111 pp.
[Bogeyman Islam] *May Arab Christians call God 'Allah'? Is Allah the Father of Jesus? How Political Parties in Germany misrepresent Islam.*

Religijos mokslas. Prizmês knyga. Siaulai (Litauen): Campus Fidus, 2004. 106 pp.
[Secular Religions] *In Latvian: Essays on Religions, Marxism, National Socialism and the devil in Art and Literature.*

Bildungspflicht statt Schulzwang. VKW/VTR/idea: Bonn et. al., 2005. 90 pp.
[Compulsory Education or Compulsary Schooling] *A scientific evaluation of homeschooling.*

Der Ablass RVB/VTR: Hamburg, 2005. 144 pp.
[The Indulgences] *History and theology of the Catholic view on indulgences.*

Die Apokryphen RVB/VTR: Hamburg, 2005. 92 pp.
[The Apocrypha] *History and theology of the Catholic view on the Apocrypha and an apology of the Protestant position.*

Thomas Schirrmacher et al. Christ und Politik: 50 Antworten auf Fragen und kritische Einwände. VKW: Bonn, 2006. 125 pp.

[Christians and Politics] *Schirrmacher and three members of parliament from Switzerland answer questions around the relation of church and state and the political involvement of Evangelicals.*

Der Segen von Ehe und Familie: Interessante Erkenntnisse aus Forschung und Statistik. VKW: Bonn, 2006. 125 pp.

[The Blessing of Marriage and Family] *Introduction to 200 scientific studies and statistics, that prove the blessing of longterm marriage and stable family.*

Multikulturelle Gesellschaft: Chancen und Gefahren. Hänssler: Holzgerlingen, 2006. 100 pp.

[Multicultural Society] *A history of multiculturalism (especially Muslims and Russian-Germans) in Germany and its political, economic and religious implications for the future of Germany.*

Die neue Unterschicht: Armut in Deutschland? Hänssler: Holzgerlingen, 2007. 120 pp.

[The New Low Cast] *A sociology of low caste people in Germany, the differences in culture to low caste people one hundred years ago, tasks for churches and the State.*

Hitlers Kriegsreligion: Die Verankerung der Weltanschauung Hitlers in seiner religiösen Begrifflichkeit und seinem Gottesbild. 2 vol. VKW: Bonn, 2007. 1220 pp.

[Hitlers Religion of War] *A research about the religious terms and thoughts in all texts and speeches of Hitler, pleading for a new way of explaining Hitler's worldview, rise and breakdown.*

Moderne Väter: Weder Waschlappen, noch Despot. Hänssler: Holzgerlingen, 2007. 96 pp.

[Modern Fathers] *Presents the result of international father research, explains the necessity of the father's involvement for his children and gives practical guidelines.*

Sheria au Roho? Trans-Africa Swahili Christian Ministries: Mwanza, Tanzania, 2007. 96 pp.

Kiswahili-Version of 'Law and Spirit' about Galatians.

Koran und Bibel: Die größten Religionen im Vergleich. Hänssler: Holzgerlingen, 2008. 96 pp.

[Quran and Bible] *Compares the differences between the Muslim of the Quran as the ‚Word of God' and the Christian view of the Bible as*

the 'Word of God'. A classic on the inspiration of the Bible.

Christenverfolgung heute. Hänssler: Holzgerlingen, 2008. 96 pp.

[The Persecution of Christians today] *Gives an overview of the persecution of Christians worldwide and presents a short theology of persecution as well political reasons for the fight for religious freedom.*

Internetpornografie. Hänssler: Holzgerlingen, 2008. 156 pp.

[Internet pornography] *Intense study of spread of pornography, its use amongst children and young people, its psychological results and dangers, including steps how to escape sex and pornography addiction.*

Russian Edition 2009

May a Christian Go to Court? The WEA Global Issues Series, Vol. 3. VKW: Bonn, 2008. 120 pp.

Essays: „Is Involvement in the Fight Against the Persecution of Christians Solely for the Benefit of Christians?", „But with gentleness and respect: Why missions should be ruled by ethics". „May a Christian Go to Court?", „Putting Rumors to Rest", „Human Rights and Christian Faith", „There Has to Be a Social Ethic".

Rassismus: Alte Vorurteile und neue Einsichten. Hänssler: Holzgerlingen, 2009. 120 pp.

[Racism] *History and scientific errors of racism*

Fundamentalismus: Wenn Religion gefährlich wird. SCM Hänssler: Holzgerlingen, 2009. 120 pp.

[Fundamentalism] *History of term, definition, examples from all religions.*

Menschenhandel: Die Rückkehr der Sklaverei. SCM Hänssler: Holzgerlingen, 2011. 106 pp.

[Human Trafficking: The Return of Slavery] *History and present situation of human trafficking including Europe, discusses legal and other reasons that prevent the fight against modern slavery.*

Responsabilitatea etica in luarea deciziilor (2011) Scriptum, Oradea (Romania), 2011. 210 pp.

Rumanian version of 'Internetpornography'.

Mafunzo Yahusuyo Uongozi wa Kanisa. Trans-Africa Swahili Christian Ministries: Mwanza, Tanzania, 2011. 127 pp.

Kiswahili-Version of 'Studies in Church Leadership'

Mateso ya Wakristo Yanatuhusu Sisi Sote.
Trans-Africa Swahili Christian Ministries:
Mwanza, Tanzania, 2011. 156 pp.
Kiswahili-Version of 'Persecution of Christians Concerns Us All'

Akutaka Ujifunze, Ufanye Kazi na Upende.
Trans-Africa Swahili Christian Ministries:
Mwanza, Tanzania, 2011. 76 pp.
Kiswahili-Version of 'God Wants You to Learn Labor and Love'

Indulgences: A History of Theology and
Reality of Indulgences and Purgatory. VKW:
Bonn, 2011. 164 pp.
History and theology of the Catholic view on indulgences.

Racism. VKW: Bonn, 2011. 100 pp.
History and scientific errors of racism

As editor (always with own contributions):

Patrick Johnstone. Handbuch für Weltmission: Gebet für die Welt. Hänssler: Neuhausen, 1987[2], newest edition 1993[6] (together with Christine Schirrmacher). 811 pp.
[Handbook on World Mission] *Adapted German version of 'Operation World', a handbook and lexicon on the situation of Christianity and missions in every country of the world.*

Gospel Recordings Language List: Liste der Sprachaufnahmen in 4.273 Sprachen. Missiologica Evangelica 4. Verlag für Kultur und Wissenschaft: Bonn, 1992. 120 pp.
List of 4273 languages in the world, in which evangelistic cassettes are available.

„Die Zeit für die Bekehrung der Welt ist reif": Rufus Anderson und die Selbständigkeit der Kirche als Ziel der Mission. Edition afem: mission scripts 3. Verlag für Kultur und Wissenschaft: Bonn, 1993. 134 pp.
[The Time of Conversion is Ripe: Rufus Anderson and The Independence of] *Articles by Schirrmacher and by theologians from the 19th century about Rufus Anderson, leading American missionary statesman, Reformed professor of missions and postmillennial theologian – together with the first translation of texts of Anderson into German.*

William Carey. Eine Untersuchung über die Verpflichtung der Christen [1792]. Edition afem: mission classics 1. Verlag für Kultur und Wissenschaft: Bonn, 1993 (together with Klaus Fiedler). 100 pp.
[An Inquire into the Means ...] *First German translation of the book by the Calvinist Baptist William Carey of 1792, with which the age of modern Protestant world missions started.*

Bibeltreue in der Offensive: Die drei Chicagoerklärungen zur biblischen Unfehlbarkeit, Hermeneutik und Anwendung. Biblia et symbiotica 2. Verlag für Kultur und Wissenschaft: Bonn, 1993[1]; 2000[2]. 90 pp.
German translation of the three Chicago-

Declarations on biblical inerrancy, hermeneutics and application.

Im Kampf um die Bibel – 100 Jahre Bibelbund. Biblia et symbiotica 6. Verlag für Kultur und Wissenschaft: Bonn, 1994 (together with Stephan Holthaus). 168 pp.
[The Batlle for the Bible] *'Festschrift' for 100 years of „Bibelbund". Articles on biblical inerrancy and on the history of the major German organization fighting higher criticism, the „Bibelbund" (Bible League), and its theological journal „Bibel und Gemeinde", edited by Schirrmacher 1988-1997.*

Eduard Böhl. Dogmatik. Hänssler Theologie. Hänssler: Neuhausen, 1995; 2nd ed.: Hamburg: RVB & Bonn: VKW, 2004. 508 pp.
[Dogmatic Theology] *A Reformed Systematic Theology from the last century edited by Thomas Schirrmacher; with a lengthy introduction on Böhl's life and work.*

Der evangelische Glaube kompakt: Ein Arbeitsbuch. Hänssler: Neuhausen, 1998; 2nd ed.: Hamburg: RVB & Bonn: VKW, 2004. 246 pp.
[The Protestant Faith in Nuce] *German translation of the Westminster Confession of Faith, adapted and with commentary and changes in Presbyterian, Congregationalist and Baptist versions.*

Werden alle gerettet? Referate der Jahrestagung 1998 des AfeM (with Klaus W. Müller). Verlag für Kultur und Wissenschaft: Bonn, 1998. 160 pp.
[Will All Be Saved?] *The proceedings of a missiological consultation on the relationship between Christianity's mission and other religions.*

The Right to Life for Every Person / Lebensrecht für jeden Menschen. Abortion – Euthanasia – Gen Technology: Proceedings of the 1st European Right to Life Forum Berlin, 1998. Abtreibung – Euthanasie – Gentechnik: Beiträge des 1. Europäischen Forums Lebens-

recht Berlin, 1999 (with Walter Schrader, Hartmut Steeb). Verlag für Kultur und Wissenschaft: Bonn, 1999. 310 pp.
Basic articles on biomedical topics, includes reports on the prolife movements in most European countries.

Kein anderer Name: Die Einzigartigkeit Jesu Christi und das Gespräch mit nichtchristlichen Religionen. Festschrift zum 70. Geburtstag von Peter Beyerhaus. Verlag für Theologie und Religionswissenschaft: Nürnberg, 1999. 470 pp.
[No Other Name: The Uniqueness of Jesus Christ ...] *Festschrift for Prof. Peter Beyerhaus, the leading evangelical authority on missions, ecumenical issues and on other religions and an evangelical elder statesmen. Covers all aspects of the relationship of Christian faith to other religions.*

Missionswissenschaft im Zeichen der Erneuerung: Ehrengabe zum 70. Geburtstag von Peter Beyerhaus. Sonderausgabe = Evangelikale Missiologie 15 (1999) Heft 2 (together with Klaus W. Müller und Christof Sauer) (1999) afem
Shorter version of the former Festschrift for mass distribution

Ausbildung als missionarischer Auftrag: Referate der Jahrestagung 1999 des AfeM (with Klaus W. Müller). Verlag für Kultur und Wissenschaft: Bonn, 2000. 210 pp.
[Theological education as World Mission] *Lectures on the relation of missions and theological education by leading representatives of theological schools, alternative programs, missions and third world churches.*

Mission in der Spannung zwischen Hoffnung, Resignation und Endzeitenthusiasmus: Referate der Jahrestagung 2000 des AfeM (together with Klaus W. Müller). Verlag für Kultur und Wissenschaft: Bonn, 2001. 240 pp.
Lectures on the relation of eschatology and missions in history and in present reality.

Märtyrer 2001 — Christenverfolgung vor allem in islamischen Ländern. (with Max Klingberg). Verlag für Kultur und Wissenschaft: Bonn, 2001. 140 pp.
[Martyrs 2001] *Documentation on the present status of persecution of Christians in Islamic countries.*

Anwalt der Liebe – Martin Bucer als Theologe und Seelsorger: Zum 450. Todestag des Reformators. Jahrbuch des Martin Bucer Seminars 1 (2001). VKW: Bonn, 2001. 160 pp.
[Advocate of Love: Martin Bucer as Theolo-

gian and Counselor] *Yearbook of the Martin Bucer Seminary on Life and Theology of the reformer Martin Bucer.*

Die vier Schöpfungsordnungen Gottes: Kirche, Staat, Wirtschaft und Familie bei Dietrich Bonhoeffer und Martin Luther. VTR: Nürnberg, 2001. 110 pp.
[The four Creation Orders] *Three lengthy essays discuss the importance of the four major creation orders family, church, work and state in the Bible, and in the work of Martin Luther and Dietrich Bonhoeffer.*

Baumeister bleibt der Herr: Festgabe zum 80. Geburtstag von Prof. Bernd Schirrmacher (with Klaus Schirrmacher und Ingrid von Torklus). VKW: Bonn, 2001. 33300 pp.
[God Stays the Master Builder] *Festschrift for Thomas Schirrmacher's father on his 80th birthday. Essays mainly concentrate on Christian education and Evangelical schools.*

A Life of Transformation: Festschrift for Colonel V. Doner. RVB International: Hamburg, 2001. 350 pp.
Festschrift for one of the giants of international Christian relief work and social involvement.

Märtyrer 2002 — Jahrbuch zur Christenverfolgung heute (with Max Klingberg). Verlag für Kultur und Wissenschaft: Bonn, 2002. 140 pp.
[Martyrs 2002] *Yearbook with documentation of the present status of persecution of Christians with special emphasize on Indonesia, Pakistan, Turkey and Vietnam.*

Patrick Johnstone. Gebet für die Welt. Hänssler: Holzgerlingen, 2003. 1010 pp.
[Prayer for the World] *Adapted German version of 'Operation World', a handbook and lexicon on the situation of Christianity and missions in every country of the world.*

Märtyrer 2003 — Jahrbuch zur Christenverfolgung heute (with Max Klingberg). Verlag für Kultur und Wissenschaft: Bonn, 2003. 180 pp.
[Martyrs 2003] *Yearbook with documentation of the present status of persecution of Christians, featuring Cuba, Japan, North Korea, Vietnam.*

Wenn Kinder zu Hause zur Schule gehen (with Thomas Mayer). VTR: Nürnberg, 2004. 260 pp.
[When Children Go to Scholl at Home] *Documentation and scientific essays on homeschooling in Germany and Europe.*

Menschenrechte für Minderheiten in Deutschland und Europa: Vom Einsatz für die Religionsfreiheit durch die Evangelische Allianz und die Freikirchen im 19. Jahrhundert (with Karl Heinz Voigt). Verlag für Kultur und Wissenschaft: Bonn, 2004. 120 pp. [Human Rights for Minorities in Germany and Europe] *Research articles on the history of the defense of religious freedom by the Evangelical Alliance in Germany and Great Britain in the 19th century.*

Herausforderung China: Ansichten, Einsichten, Aussichten: Eine Dokumentation von idea und China Partner (with Konrad Brandt). Verlag für Kultur und Wissenschaft: Bonn, 2004. 214 pp. *[Challenge China] A collection of reports, lectures and opinion on the situation of religions and the Christian faith in China, combining reports on persecution and reports on huge progress for public Christianity.*

Europa Hoffnung geben: Dokumentation (with Thomas Mayer). VTR: Nürnberg, 2004. 197 pp. *[To Give Hope to Europe] Lectures of a theological conference in Budapest by John-Warwick Montgomery, Thomas K. Johnston, William Mikler, Bernhard Knieß on the future of Europe and how to defend the gospel of hope in Europe.*

Märtyrer 2004 – Das Jahrbuch zur Christenverfolgung heute. (with Max Klingberg). Verlag für Kultur und Wissenschaft: Bonn, 2004. 160 pp. *[Martyrs 2004] Yearbook with documentation of the present status of persecution of Christians, with two longer studies on the situation in Nigeria and Iran.*

Tabuthema Tod? Vom Sterben in Würde. (with Roland Jung, Frank Koppelin). Jahrbuch des Martin Bucer Seminars 4 (2004). VKW: Bonn, 2004. 220 pp. *[Death as Taboo?] 8 major Evangelical ethicists discuss topics around counseling seriously ill and dying people, death, euthanasia, counseling of relatives.*

Mission verändert – Mission verändert sich / Mission Transformes – Mission is Transformed: Festschrift für Klaus Fiedler. (with Christof Sauer). Nürnberg: VTR & Bonn: VKW, 2005. 572 pp. *Festschrift for African missionary and doyen of African and German mission history Klaus Fiedler.*

Märtyrer 2005 – Das Jahrbuch zur Christenverfolgung heute. (mit Max Kling-

berg). Verlag für Kultur und Wissenschaft: Bonn, 2005. 170 pp. *[Martyrs 2005] Yearbook with documentation of the present status of persecution of Christians, featuring Nigeria, China, Indonesia, Vietnam, Turkey.*

Ein Maulkorb für Christen? Juristen nehmen Stellung zum deutschen Antidiskriminierungsgesetz und ähnlichen Gesetzen in Europa und Australien. (with Thomas Zimmermanns). VKW: Bonn, 2005 *[A Muzzle for Christians?] Studies in religious hate laws, antidiscrimination laws and their influence on Christian communities.*

Scham- oder Schuldgefühl? Die christliche Botschaft angesichts von schuld- und schamorientierten Gewissen und Kulturen. Verlag für Kultur und Wissenschaft: Bonn, 2005. 99 pp. *[Shame- and Guiltfeeling] This study explains the difference between shame- and guilt-oriented cultures and shows, that the 'Biblical' message emphasizes shame and guilt equally and thus can be applied to cultures in the West, the East, in modern and in Third World cultures.*

Scham- und Schuldorientierung in der Diskussion: Kulturanthropologische, missiologische und theologische Einsichten (mit Klaus W. Müller). VTR: Nürnberg & VKW: Bonn, 2006 *[Shame- and Guilt orientation] A selection of experts from all continents on the difference between shame- and guilt-oriented cultures and its implications for world missions.*

Familienplanung – eine Option für Christen?. Verlag für Kultur und Wissenschaft: Bonn, 2006. 170 pp. *[Family Planning – An Option for Christians?] A Protestant view of family planning.*

Märtyrer 2006 – Das Jahrbuch zur Christenverfolgung heute. (with Max Klingberg und Ron Kubsch). Verlag für Kultur und Wissenschaft: Bonn, 2006. 170 pp. *[Martyrs 2006] Yearbook with documentation of the present status of persecution of Christians, concentrating on Iran, Iraq, Turkey and North Korea.*

Martin Bucer als Vorreiter der Mission. VKW: Bonn & VTR: Nürnberg, 2006. 110 pp. *[Martin Bucer as Forerunner of World Mission] Essays from the 19th century to the present on Martin Bucer being the only Reformer arguing in favor of world mission.*

Märtyrer 2007 – Das Jahrbuch zur Christenverfolgung heute. (with Max Kling-

berg und Ron Kubsch). Verlag für Kultur und Wissenschaft: Bonn, 2007. 200 pp.
[Martyrs 2007] *Yearbook with documentation of the present status of persecution of Christians, concentrating on India, Turkey, Iraq, Indonesia and Germany.*

HIV und AIDS als christliche Herausforderung 1: Grundsätzliche Erwägungen. (mit Kurt Bangert). Verlag für Kultur und Wissenschaft: Bonn, 2008. 211 pp.
[HIV and AIDS as Christian Challenge 1: General Discussion] *Essay on how the Christian church should react to HIV and AIDS and how it does react. Published together with World Vision Germany.*

HIV und AIDS als christliche Herausforderung 2: Aus der praktischen Arbeit. (mit Kurt Bangert). Verlag für Kultur und Wissenschaft: Bonn, 2008. 280 pp.
[HIV and AIDS as Christian Challenge 2: What Is Done and Can Be Done] *Volume 2 of the same*

Märtyrer 2008 – Das Jahrbuch zur Christenverfolgung heute. (with Max Klingberg und Ron Kubsch). VKW: Bonn, 2008. 180 pp.
[Martyrs 2008] *Yearbook with documentation of the present status of persecution of Christians, concentrating on Iran, Egypt, Afghanistan, Germany, Vietnam, Turkey.*

Johannes Calvin. Christliche Glaubenslehre: Erstausgabe der 'Institutio' von 1536. VKW: Bonn, 2008
New German edition of the first edition of John Calvin's Institutes (1536) with lengthy introduction.

Märtyrer 2009 – Das Jahrbuch zur Christenverfolgung heute. (with Max Klingberg und Ron Kubsch). VKW: Bonn, 2009. 270 pp.
[Martyrs 2009] *Yearbook with documentation of the present status of persecution of Christians, concentrating on India, Eritrea, Yemen.*

Glaube nur im Kämmerlein? Zum Schutz religiöser Freiheitsrechte konvertierter Asylbewerber. (with Friedemann Burkhardt). VKW/Idea: Bonn, 2009. 100 pp.
[Faith only in the Chamber?] *The protection of religious freedom rights for asylum seekers in Germany having converted from Islam to Christianity.*

Die Aufnahme verfolgter Christen aus dem Irak in Deutschland: Die Vorgeschichte eines ungewöhnlichen Beschlusses im Spiegel der Presse. VKW/Idea: Bonn, 2009. 130 pp.
[The entry of persecuted Christians from Iraq into Germany] *Press articles during 2008 documenting the decision of the German government and the EU to accept thousands of Christians refugees from Iraq.*

Der Kampf gegen die weltweite Armut – Aufgabe der Evangelischen Allianz? Zur biblisch-theologischen Begründung der Micha-Initiative. (with Andreas Kusch). VKW/Idea: Bonn, 2009. 230 pp.
[The fight against poverty – task of the Evangelical Alliance?] *Essays by theologians, missiologists, activists etc. in favour of the MICAH initiative of the World Evangelical Alliance.*

Tough-Minded Christianity: Honoring the Legacy of John Warwick Montgomery. (with William Dembski). (2009) B&H Academic Publ.: Nashville (TN). 830 pp.
Large Festschrift with essays by many major Evangelical theologians and lawyers.

Calvin and World Mission: Essays. VKW: Bonn, VTR: Nürnberg, 2009. 204 pp.
Collection of essays from 1882 to 2002.

Märtyrer 2010 – Das Jahrbuch zur Christenverfolgung heute. (with Max Klingberg und Ron Kubsch). VKW: Bonn, 2010. 200 pp.
[Martyrs 2010] *Yearbook with documentation of the present status of persecution of Christians, concentrating on China, India, Nigeria, Indonesia, and the German parliament and Catholic martyrology.*

Märtyrer 2011 – Das Jahrbuch zur Christenverfolgung heute. (with Max Klingberg und Ron Kubsch). VKW: Bonn, 2011. 300 pp.
[Martyrs 2011] *Yearbook with documentation of the present status of persecution of Christians, concentrating on the Arab World, Egypt, Eritrea, Nigeria, China and Europe.*

www.ingramcontent.com/pod-product-compliance
Lightning Source LLC
Chambersburg PA
CBHW070254290326
41930CB00041B/2527